The New Mentality

Books by *John Charles Cooper*
Published by THE WESTMINSTER PRESS

The New Mentality
Radical Christianity and Its Sources
The Roots of the Radical Theology

The
New
Mentality

by John Charles Cooper

The Westminster Press
Philadelphia

STANDARD BOOK NO. 664–24855–1
LIBRARY OF CONGRESS CATALOG CARD NO. 69–16304

PUBLISHED BY THE WESTMINSTER PRESS ®
PHILADELPHIA, PENNSYLVANIA

PRINTED IN THE UNITED STATES OF AMERICA

*This book is dedicated to my children
in the hope that in them the new mentality
may come to the fullest consciousness
and result in the practice of
universal love*

Preface

A new form of consciousness is stirring within us. Rising from within ourselves, rising up from the unconscious depths, rising more ominously than ever before for things as-they-now-are. More ominously even than the specter of Communism or of slave revolt that moved across the face of Europe and America in the past.

This new way of looking at the world is no mere variant on an older philosophical mode. The reactionary critics of the young and the young-in-spirit miss the whole issue if they see the new consciousness as only the older liberalism or the old radicalism of the left come into being in contemporary dress.

And the new mentality is not just the evolved (or devolved) *Weltanschauung* of the old Adam—of modern, historical man. Those who speak of the creature who bears this new state of consciousness as "postmodern" and "posthistorical" do so with justification. Why? Because the distinctiveness and the radical differentness of this new form of sensibility is different in species from the older frameworks of thought. In the new mentality we see the similarities and differences that mark off a new development of man. The bearer of this new consciousness is a new creature—perhaps the new creature foreseen by Nietzsche as the "higher man." For we are in the presence of that event which so many natural scientists (as well as theologians) have declared impossible (or at least, not yet observed): an evolutionary transformation, a new step in the phylogenetic history of man.

This is a broad claim. On what basis can we intelligently claim that man—just now, as it were—has evolved? Only on the basis of the pragmatic test of Charles Sanders Peirce (1839–1914), who, as well as William James and John Dewey, taught us how to make our ideas clear. Peirce's pragmatic method enables us to clarify our ideas (in this regard and in all others) by extending the experimental method of the physical sciences into the field of philosophical and theological discussion. Briefly put, Peirce held that ideas are different in meaning only when they make an objective difference in *conduct*. Thus, a description of the conduct of those whom we have designated as "the bearers of the new mentality" ought to provide sufficient ground for judging whether they are the same or different from the race of beings called "men" up to our own time.

As Peirce stated his maxim: "Consider what effects, that might conceivably have practical bearings, we conceive the object of our conception to have. Then, our conception of these effects is the whole of our conception of the object."[1] In other words, "our idea of anything is our idea of its sensible effects."[2]

Peirce is a helpful guide in this regard, for he also observed (in reference to spiritual affairs):

No concept, not even those of mathematics, is absolutely precise; and some of the most important for everyday use are extremely vague. Nevertheless, our instinctive beliefs involving such concepts are far more trustworthy than the best established results of science, if these be precisely understood.[3]

In this book we will follow our "instinctive beliefs" as well as the results of sociological observations and philosophical reflection. The results of the new mentality are with us—all we must do is to untangle the threads that make it up.

The author wishes to acknowledge with gratitude the Research and Creativity Grant given by the Lutheran Church in America and Newberry College for the purpose of researching and writing this book.

J. C. C.

Eastern Kentucky University
Richmond, Kentucky

Contents

Contents

You yourself are all that has preceded
and precedes you in history,
and it only depends upon your
grasping it with your consciousness.

—*Adolf von Harnack,* Über die Sicherheit

The New Mentality

Minds and Mentalities

*O*NE of the easiest ways to understand the meaning of evolution with reference to the coming into being of man is to consider the origin of man to be that moment somewhere in time past when a humanoid became self-aware. In brief, the distinction between man and beast lies in the distinctive mentality of each, not in the physical appearance. What made man man was a new mentality that had not existed prior to that period some one hundred thousand years ago or more when the self-awareness and inner and outer curiosity of a new species began to leave records of its new thought world in the form of graves, cave paintings, and implements. The era of the chipped-stone tools signalized the "creation" of man as such, man the toolmaker, man the cooker of food, man the artist, and man the religious being—since only a religious being would bury its dead.

The intellectual method of describing the course of human history in terms of world outlooks or mind-sets is probably outdated. Modern historians and philosophers have become aware of the great similarities between what were once considered different types of world views. We know now that the so-called medieval mind was not so very different from the mind of Renaissance man. We have come to recognize, through the accumulation of detailed studies, that changes in world views take place over long periods of time; gradually, so that several generations of men include within their own outlooks elements of an older mind-set in creative tension with a new way of looking at the world. Perhaps the custom of speaking of "the classical mind" and "the medieval mind" is no longer followed because many cultural critics and intellectual historians have too glibly designated certain patterns of world interpretation as a "mind," when such patterns only show different philosophical predispositions. To be sure, we are well rid of the habit of speaking of "the mind of the South," "the Japanese mind," and other overly formal names given to what are actually "minority reports" within a general "mentality" which characterizes a race and time as a major segment of world history. On the other hand, it seems increasingly more necessary to understand various sharp divergencies of outlook and temper, and, more importantly, of hope, affection, and belief, between one group of people—generally belonging to one generation or age group—and another generation which has usually been the "younger generation." However, membership in the "younger" generation seems to be more a state of mind than a state of age. For example, Paul Tillich at age seventy-nine was younger in spirit and outlook than many of the students in their twenties who sat in his seminars.

Not every decade brings a "younger" generation into the public eye which shows itself completely out of temper with its parents. In point of fact, most of recorded history shows one generation following another with the chronic restlessness of youth but, overall, with relative smoothness. Throughout the several centuries that make up the Middle Ages we find that most young people fitted into the world view of their elders quite comfortably. While this was not usually the case for the students at the University of Paris and in other educational centers, this in no way invalidates our generalization, as students made up a very fractional part of the population of Europe. When we look at the ancient and still-living "primitive" societies, we discover that the rising generation is completely absorbed in the world view of the older group through the myth and ritual of initiation. But this generally smooth process has not been true of Western civilization during the last seventy-five years. Increasingly, the values and even the facts believed to be true by the older generation have been challenged by the young. Mores, moral codes, patriotism, theology—all have been questioned, shaken, often refuted, and many times spurned by youth. But there is a significant difference from the student high jinks of other periods: these young people do not necessarily readopt the older values when they mature. This is not to say that some people in every generation do not return to older forms of thought, or even that others never go through such a rebellion at all. Here, as always in objective reporting, we are dealing with the margin, the margin that is made up of that active group of people who make things happen in the world because they are interested in the world and therefore commit themselves to the understanding of and the enjoying of the world about them. This group of doers, of men and women of the deed as well as of thought, has been growing increasingly more radical as the years have passed in the twentieth century, and the signs are such that we must expect a continuation of their radicality in the future.

It has been said that the world is made up basically of only two kinds of people: those who make things happen and those who have things happen to them. The past seventy-five years have shown a remarkable double-edged growth of the activistic group: one growing edge of this group being the increase in size of that group which can make things happen by the growth of democracy and the liberation of millions of people from colonial rule; the other growing edge being the increase in the power of the active person to cause things to happen through the mastery of electricity, the gasoline engine, the power of the atom, through space research and the development of modern electronic devices and communication instruments. We may observe, then, that there has been an external, extensive growth of the active population, and an internal, intensive growth in the power available to the activist for the changing of the world. This combination of intensive and extensive increments of power available to decisive power-wielding groups is the source of the rapid technological progress and swift change of fashion in philosophy and political life in the twentieth century.

We see the new mentality reflected in the optimistic planning of the scientific community to conquer space, reach the moon, produce food and fresh water from the sea, and otherwise allocate the world's resources for the benefit of a rising population as well as in the new morality that stresses individual responsibility along with the new theology that has jettisoned the traditional comforts of theology for an optimistic realism based on man's potentiality. This new mentality is basically a gnosisolatry. By the term "gnosisolatry"—a neologism coined by this writer —I mean the worship of knowledge as the power that creates and maintains human society. In some men gnosisolatry is also the worship or veneration of the industrialized nation as the source of all good and is a larger edition of scientism, an unquestioned faith in scientific progress as man's way to salvation. However, gnosisolatry is not only the veneration of knowledge, nor only the veneration of the technological aspect of society. Rather, it is a natural emotive quality that accompanies the sense of history (called man's modern attitude of "historicness" in my book *The Roots of the Radical Theology*[1]) that grows out of the invigorating sense of power that discoveries in all the sciences from psychology to physics have given man.

However, the chief elements that make up that pattern of world outlook which I describe and define in this book as the new mentality of our era are the influence of the Christian humanism of the nineteenth century in the West, on the one hand, and the rise of human brutality on the other, growing out of the misuse of science in the development of weapons, both physical and psychological, and their extensive use in the wars of the twentieth century. These two trends or tendencies are not unrelated, but have grown out of a common veneration of knowledge, education, and scientific research. The devotion to principle, taught by Christianity and humanism, demonically swayed into ideology and nationalism, provided the reason for using—and the courage to use—the horrible weapons, from machine guns to poison gas to nuclear weapons (which only a supposedly Christian country has used), that research made available to the true believer.

The new mentality is the result of the convergence of the rising human sensitivity, which both Christian humanism and the development of psychology and sociology made possible, and the horror and pessimism that resulted from the development and actual use of modern weapons. The new mentality is a paradoxical or at least dialectical attitude toward the world— it is made up of equal parts of admiration for hero figures such as Albert Schweitzer, a man of supreme intellect and great knowledge who sacrificed the advantages of modern culture in order to serve man, and of abhorrence of the destruction of Hiroshima and Nagasaki by the application of the most advanced techniques and refined knowledge of modern science.

Two Kinds of Human Beings

We have mentioned the phenomena of the growth of an activistic, optimistic, and intellectual minority of human beings in the twentieth century who are increasingly becoming more powerful in the formation of public opinion and the swaying of public policy in the Western countries as well as becoming increasingly radical vis-à-vis political, economic, social, and religious issues. Jack Newfield has written about the younger section of this world-affirming group and called them "a prophetic minority."[2] He says that it is "a prophetic minority [which] creates each generation's legend. It is the active radicals of the new left who are defining the generation of the 1960's."[3]

It is not necessary to limit the term "radical activist" or the title "prophetic minority" to the very young people living in the second half of the twentieth century. As I have pointed out in my earlier book,[4] there has always been such an activistic, creative, and critical prophetic minority in Western culture from the beginnings of Greek civilization to the atomic age. The generation of men who do not have things happen to them but who make things happen also cannot be limited, as some of the more super-ficial younger thinkers have declared, to those under thirty. The prophetic minority is made up of all those of all ages who have, in the words of Johann Gottlieb Fichte (1762–1814), "raised themselves to the full feeling of their freedom and of absolute independence."[5]

Fichte, writing long ago, said this of man: "Attend to thy-self; turn thy glance away from all that surrounds thee and upon thine own innermost self. Such is the first demand which philos-ophy makes of its disciples. We speak of nothing that is without thee, but wholly of thyself."[6] In other words, Fichte saw that the modern problem is one of an evolution of a new form of mentality or of self-consciousness rather than an exterior prob-lem of men's living together or conquering the earth. The real lines of division do not run between men in their age, sex, lan-guage, national, race, or economic differences but rather be-tween individuals within all these categories who exhibit either an old mentality that is dying out or a new mentality that is just now in the modern era evolving out of the old. In a real way, all modern problems can be termed instances of the major prob-lem of reaching a new stage in human evolution. The fact that there have been examples of this new species of human mentality running back certainly to six centuries before Christ, and per-haps much farther back, does not in the least damage our evolu-tionary theory, for twenty-six hundred years is but a moment in the evolutionary history of the human race. Certainly, too, re-cent findings of paleontologists in Africa seem to indicate that two species of early men lived side by side until one simply out-lasted the other because, for whatever reason (probably because of the surviving species' flexibility), one group disappeared and the other remained. The fact that the members of what I have called the new mentality are more flexible in their response to the problems of science and civilization in contrast to the reac-tionary nature of their critics would seem to indicate that if his-tory repeats itself, evolution will simply take care of our present problems over the long run. It is the devilish destructiveness that can occur in the short run, however, that the reasonable person must concern himself with. Unfortunately, the old mentality is scientific enough to bring about the destruction of the entire human experiment if the new mentality is not recognized as the "wisdom of nature" that points toward the sole hope for racial survival.

However, the new man who has arisen in our day bearing a new mentality and exhibiting a new morality has to define himself, that is, must search for his identity before he can attempt to work out a program whereby he can bring a reasoned peace to this alienated planet.

Groping for a Life Space

Man, like many other animals, requires a life space, or *Lebensraum,* in which to move, grow, feed, reproduce, create. The mildest of creatures, such as squirrels, will fight to defend their territory around a nut tree while some herds of large animals possess, use, and defend a territory of hundreds of square miles. Man, while living, also needs more than 6 x 6 x 3 feet of geographic space—although the exact amount of *Lebensraum* is a matter of debate. Let us say that every human being needs at least that much life space which allows him to be psychically, not just physically, comfortable.

Erik Erikson has written graphically of the search for identity, that which is the life project of every human life, in *Identity and the Life Cycle,*[7] and he has applied his theories to a historical character in his *Young Man Luther.*[8] Erikson, correctly, I believe, sees the period of late adolescence and early adulthood as the time when the human being must find its own sense of identity. On this basis we can readily recognize that most of the persons who are undergoing the struggles and protests taken together that we call the new mentality are undergoing struggles of identity also.

The life pattern of each young person is like a graph demonstrating his struggle to find such a psychic life space. Each mem-

ber of the generation that is producing the new mentality is seeking to find a place within himself as well as without where he
can be himself, or, in the new argot, where he can "do his own
thing."

This life space must not be too restrictive, nor must it be too
large. A small psychic space chokes down the *élan vital*. On the
other hand, too large an area allows the self to become lost—as
in the case of the user of drugs who literally loses himself in the
unbounded psychic area of a stimulated imagination.

A great deal of the almost revolutionary activity of young
people from every class of society in the past decade can be
attributed to their inner drives to carve out a life space in which
they can become themselves and in which they can escape a general destruction of civilization. Dropping out of school, going to
San Francisco, protesting the war in Vietnam, refusing to study
business or science, switching from business administration to
philosophy or Oriental religions, thinking about the ministry,
joining the Peace Corps, burning down a building, smoking pot,
or taking LSD; or for a change of pace, volunteering for the
Army, or getting married—all these are ways in which young
people today are trying to carve out both a physical and a
psychic life space for themselves. Youth today seem to feel, and
may be justified in their feeling, that the life of their elders is
not a real life at all. One gets the impression from the music of
the Beatles and the day-glow paint of recent op-art posters that
these are very religious people looking for the life that is life
indeed. They seem to be searching in Zen, in the latest guru
who comes from India, as well as in drug-taking, for the kind of
newness of life that the Gospel of John reports that Jesus promised men. It is evidently a failure of the first order on the part
of the church that it has lost the power to appeal to these
searchers, for they seem to be groping in their music and in their
art for precisely the kinds of answers that primitive Christianity
gave to men. Perhaps a description of an encounter with some
of these young people will illustrate what I mean.

Morality in the "Let It All Hang Out" Generation

Let us imagine that we are visiting a college campus of the present time.[9] We cross the quadrangle and pass the classroom buildings. We approach the dormitories and turn into one of the men's dorms. We are struck by the dinginess and disorder that we see in one of the dorm rooms. All at once our own college days come rushing back. We recognize our own past with a flash —the dirty socks on the chair, the toothpaste tube on the littered desk, the girlie photos and beer signs on the walls. All this is familiar—only the turtleneck sweater on the bed and the motorcycle boots by the window seem strange. But then we look at the books crammed on the shelves, and we look past the "Playmate" pictures to the antiwar and antiestablishment cartoons. Hermann Hesse's *Siddhartha* and *Steppenwolf* stand side by side with Dylan Thomas. An album cover of one of The Byrds' early folk-rock records shares a shelf with *Medieval Philosophy*. Cartoons poke fun—a macabre fun—at the war in Vietnam: "War is good business, invest your son." L.B.J.'s photo covers a dart board festooned with the legend, "He has an Alamo mentality."

This is the weird amalgam of the political hippiness and the "skuzziness" of the dropped-out hippie that forms the *Zeitgeist* of the present college generation.[10] An existentialist could go wild over the abundance of paradoxes found in this subculture. A set of Confederate flags hangs side by side with a record jacket featuring a Negro performer. An ROTC uniform hangs in a closet across from the antiwar drawings. Two empty whiskey bottles share a top shelf with a devotional book. All is out of any recognized order. All is chaos, all is in flux—which is to say that the young people who live in this room are children of our time.

Looking more closely, we find that a true morality can be discerned within this living flux. Talking to these representatives of the majority under thirty, we find that they hold an inchoate but sensitively felt system of morality—quite at odds with the recognized or civic morality of the middle class in our day.

"You don't hurt anyone, you try to leave one another in peace"—the records cry out, the books insist, the young people articulate. "You don't turn one another in, you don't sell the people out to the establishment," screams out the sympathy these people feel for the underdog. "Make love, not war"; "the only real pornography is violence," these youth insist.

The photos of the girl friends in their miniskirts bring to mind the journals' much talked of "sexual revolution." Upon deeper investigation we find, however, that the current sexual situation among the young seems to be more of a reformation than a revolution. This relaxation of anxiety over formalization, this lack of concern for full security, is the attitude described by the phrase, "Let it all hang out." This freedom from fear and concern is also the source of the envious anger and malice of the older generation against the younger. This liberation from existential *Angst* and optimistic openness for a nonguaranteed future is the one possession of the young today, and the supreme content of their sexual revolution, while being the sharpest threat to the egos of the rest of us.

The same relaxation of anxiety and lack of concern for future security carries over to the attitude of most young people toward war, politics, and the racial crisis. The turned-on young person simply cannot take seriously the beat of the war drum calling us to hold back the Red tide in Asia or to make political and social points at home. Most young people simply do not believe in the imminent danger of the Red menace. All we learn about the Russians seems to show us people like ourselves; all we (with difficulty) learn about the Red Chinese makes us think them justified in much of their hostility toward America.

The coincidence of the twin themes of increased sexual fulfillment and desire for peaceful coexistence finds beautiful expression in the button legend, "Make love, not war." These twin streams taken together also remind us that much aggression is due to sexual frustration.

The Historic Self-consciousness of Postmodern Man

John Cage has written: "Our minds are changing . . . from an unrealistic concern with a nonexistent status quo to a courageous seeing things in movement, life as revolution. History is one revolution after another."[11] If it is true that we live in a post-Christian age, a time when the church and its symbols no longer speak to the deepest concerns and anxieties of most Western men, it is also true to say that we live in a post-Marxian era—the symbols of the revolutionary proletariat are as silent and archaic as the symbol of the blood of the lamb. The revolt that burns like a bed of charcoals in our inner cities and parades in psychedelic colors across every campus is not the October Revolution warmed over, but a raw, utter, complete and total rejection of mid-twentieth-century culture and its philosophical core—including the very concept of twentieth-century revolt itself. The revolt of postmodern man is compounded of many things: a Franciscan strain of Christian ethical fundamentalism, a Nietzschean rejection of or transvaluation of all contemporary ethical positions, a delight in the developing knowledge psychology has gained about the mind and human behavior, and an existentialist vision of man-alone defining his most basic self, joined to the moral and social outrage of a Karl Marx and an Erich Fromm. The revolt of the postmodern man represents a change from quantity to quality, for it has ushered in a new mentality that does not transgress moral codes but demands a new morality; does not demand social reform but calls for urban guerrilla warfare if human needs are not met; and does not content itself with saying, "Get out of Vietnam," but calls for the victory of the Viet Cong. This is the "tough revolt."

There is, in short, a new man in twentieth-century America—and Europe—and we will never understand his mentality if we judge him by the models of even the quite recent past.

Man's Alienation from Traditional Symbols

O N every side the commentators on the status of life in the Western world today remark upon the erosion or even the death of the symbols that communicate and vivify the insights and meanings that make up the Western tradition. It is common to speak of the "death of God," which is a supremely clear declaration of the loss of contact on the part of Western man with the deepest roots of his hereditary culture. It is also a popular pastime to observe that morality is dying or dead and that the symbols incorporated in the flag, the national anthem, and other insignia of race and soil have lost much of their power to move men to self-sacrifice. Why should this be the case? What are symbols? Are they necessary elements in human life? Let us investigate what symbols are and what they do in human culture.

What Symbols Are

In the most basic sense, symbols are the currency of human communication. Symbols form the psychological background of the words and allusions and give color and concreteness to the expressions of human thought in speech and writing. Symbols are also the background of the nonverbal intracommunication of men's minds. Examples of symbols are the Christian cross, the Marxists' Red star, the peace movement's "Ban the Bomb" symbol as well as the image of the wise man, the father, and such things as snakes, trees, swords, and other ageless representations of masculinity.

Symbols are often confused with signs. However, the symbol should be kept distinct from the sign (such as the plus sign, or a red light at a crossroads), because signs are purely arbitrary, while symbols have a much more complex relationship to man's mind and to that which is believed to be symbolized in any particular symbol.

Paul Tillich has discussed this complex relationship of man and symbol under six general insights.[1] We shall here only mention Tillich's analysis of symbols, but an acceptance of this analysis underlies what is said about symbols in the rest of this book. Tillich holds that only through the symbol can man express his ultimate concern; that is, only in the form of expression which reaches deep into man's mind and which stretches out socially across a human group can he express the deepest urges and highest goals he recognizes in life. Only something like the cross or the Red star or the Star of David is deep enough and broad enough to signify the meaning of a man's life.

Since symbols express the deepest meanings that men of a historical group have experienced, it follows that symbols point beyond themselves, or we might say through themselves to something other than themselves. Just what the status of this other is is a moot question, but it is clear that the cross points to and, indeed, conveys to man something more than an instrument of execution. In the same way, the Red star or the hammer and sickle conveys more than a reference to workers or objects in the night sky. Apparently symbols direct us to feelings and thoughts that lie too deep for conscious verbal communication. Only by way of the symbol can we refer to these deep levels of human experience, and apart from these symbols speech about such dimensions of life is barren.

This last remark brings us to Tillich's insight that symbols open up for us dimensions of both exterior and interior reality that are otherwise closed to us. Apart from symbol usage our lives would be less rich and broad, and we would regress from the level of development of adult humanity to the status of infants.

In reference to the problem of the origin of symbols, there are two major theses. According to C. G. Jung,[2] symbols are inherent in man, coming up out of man's "racial consciousness." Men recognize symbols because man has used them for so long that they have become part of his subconscious mental equipment. According to Tillich, symbols are produced by ecstatic experiences in which man receives revelations of the Divine Ground of all life. The point is that symbols cannot be invented but are born out of the life experiences of historical groups. The meaning of symbols as understood by this writer—and therefore the definition of the term "symbol" used throughout this book—includes the insight that symbols are born out of random historical events in the lives of historical groups of human beings such as tribes, nations, and churches. Such symbols are not invented but discovered, for the symbol is the expression in finite form of an awareness on the part of mankind of the underlying processes of life. The awareness of these life processes and of the reoccurring patterns of these processes in human experience becomes particularized in a concrete event such as a cross or a star, so that men will be able to refer back to this insight in later times.

A final insight into the nature of symbols is that they can and do die. This means that they become inappropriate to the expression of man's deepest insights and feelings and hence gradually grow unavailable for purposes of inner and outer communication. An example of a symbol that has died would be the figures of Baal that were prominent in the Middle East three thousand years ago. It is important to note that symbols die not because of skepticism and criticism but because they no longer express man's feelings and insights into reality.

It should be clear by now that we do not attribute any supernatural qualities to symbols, whatever their function. But neither do we limit them to some opposite field called the "natural." Our description is intended to be phenomenological: a record made without prejudice to the inner experience of the transaction between man and man by way of the vehicle of meaning we call the symbol. Symbols do not need to be explained; they just are.

The only evidence for or against the truth of a symbol is the empirical measurement of its power to evoke in men feelings of reverence and trust or to provoke men to acts of courage and resoluteness. In order to judge the intelligence or lack of it involved in adhering to a symbol or symbol system such as the cross (and a variety of Christianity) or the Red flag (and a variety of Marxism), one need only look for the vitality or lack of it in the men who claim loyalty to those symbols. There is no other test. And yet we are not caught in a mystic circle. We are not without the possibility of making at least one literal statement about symbols. We are not lost in pan-symbolism which sees everything as a symbol and cannot speak of any dimension of reality beyond, above, beneath, or even alongside the symbol. We are not left with phenomenalism which must deny any level of reality beyond the phenomenal world of sense experience. We can say precisely that symbols are locations or forms in which men become aware of the power of life that drives everything on through the dimension of time. The symbol is true if it conveys this power just as a water pipe is functional if it conveys water to us from the river. If the symbol brings vitality and life into our lives, it is true, it is good, and it is useful. If it does not bring such vitality to us, then the symbol is dead.

How the Chief Symbol of Faith Died

Symbols function as vehicles and containers for forms of feeling and human sensitivity. Through the use of symbols men can picture for themselves, on both the subconscious and conscious levels, the deepest and basically inexpressible feelings they have about themselves and the world. But symbols can do more than this, while they are "living"—that is, while they are active and effective; they can put limits on man. By limits we mean that symbols which genuinely participate in the historically significant events of a man's human group can provide a sense of fitness and obligation for man by defining what can and cannot be thought and done. In the basic sense those actions and ideas which are considered civilized or cultured are precisely the ideas and actions permissible and possible through the communicative powers of symbols.

Symbols that are alive define what is; that is, what can be recognized by the human mind as existing and effective and inform us as to what is not by directing our attention away from certain elements that make up the universe by defining (by reason of their structure) what can be and what cannot be thought.

In the same way that the symbols of discourse with reference to physical things limit us, so too do symbols of value and ethics. Our sense of the fitness of things, our ideas of obligation, duty, and the ought also define for us what is to be considered ethical without any further investigation of whether or not our actions really are conducive to the betterment of life. Indeed, persons who no longer think they believe in the teachings of the church often continue to believe that religious symbols are "good." For example, many modern men do not believe in eternal life and some do not believe in God, but there are few men who go on to criticize such symbols as being harmful to the human race, although it may very well be true that at least some religious symbols are harmful to man's best interests. Amazingly enough, if there is such harm in religion it is usually religious people who point it out. The work of Karl Barth and of Paul Tillich is illustrative of this. However, one very sharp criticism of religion did come from an enemy of religion, Sigmund Freud. Freud clearly stated that the whole religious impulse was neurotic. The truth must lie somewhere between the affirmation of all religious symbols on the one hand and the condemnation of all of them on the other.

The symbol God did put limits on man when it was alive for the majority of human beings. The history of Western civilization reveals the humanizing service which belief in God played in Western development. At times the only check upon the destructive impulse of Western man was the fear of God. There are still men living today upon whom theism exercises such an influence. Part of the criticism of Communism over the last fifty years has been directed toward the lack of restraint by a transcendent check upon Communist programs.

The use of the symbol God defines certain types of behavior and psychic responses that were appropriate and available to man. The symbols of the ultimate source of value and of the all-knowing judge also define, for healthy minds, certain kinds of destructive behavior that are thereby rendered inappropriate to human beings.

The high symbol of God once gave meaning to the image or model that man had of himself and gave meaning to the model of the world by which man lived. In a real way when mankind accepted God it could be said with the poet that God was in his heaven and all was right with the world. God functioned as the Other over against which man defined himself. God and his spiritual realm bounded the world of the senses and gave shape to man's universe. One can readily see the reticence of Western man in giving up this meaningful symbol. Western history after the Renaissance reveals one philosophical and scientific attempt after another to "make room for God" in the developing modern world view. Descartes made God's existence as firm as his own on the basis of radical self-doubt; Newton found that he needed God to explain the regularity of the motions of the heavenly bodies. Bishop Berkeley found that only the existence of a God who perceived us made our existence possible; John Locke, who found that knowledge was empirical, still declared Christianity to be reasonable. The Diests, Schelling, Hegel, and Kant in their various ways found that there was meaning in the world because of the symbol God. With the coming of Nietzsche and the skepticism and atheism of the late nineteenth and early twentieth centuries a crisis in meaning appeared. We are still living in the midst of that crisis.

The Appropriateness and Availability of Symbols

We must explain what we mean by symbolic appropriateness and availability. By appropriateness we mean a symbol's usefulness for our communicating with one another. An appropriate symbol is rooted in a stratum of the conscious and/or subconscious mind that is actively engaged in the interpretation of meanings on the part of a large group of individuals at a given historical time. It is obvious that different strata of the conscious and subconscious minds of human beings, both individually and as groups, are active or "alive" at different times. An illustration of the active quality of different aspects or strata of the mind is the tendency of certain things to become fads for a time and then drop out of general interest. We have witnessed the very active quality of the "death of God" movement in theology and are now going through a stage when it is less lively and is being replaced by the "theology of hope" and the Christian-Marxist dialogue. We remember the popularity of dances and fashions that once had the attention of millions and now are as dead as the fads of ancient Rome. Of course, religious symbols and other elements of the human world view are of a higher order than fads, but they too have their periods of growth and decline. Symbols, Paul Tillich reminded us, like the men who use them and the nations of men who are formed by them, are born, live, and die.

To say that a symbol is nonappropriate means that the symbol appeals to a stratum of man's conscious and/or subconscious mind that has been surpassed or abandoned. Therefore an old or dead symbol finds no root or grappling place in the mind.

To speak of a symbol as being available simply means that there are some symbols in existence that do strike roots in an appropriate or functioning stratum of the mind. If we live today in a period when there are no symbols that seem appropriate and helpful to us in our search for meaning and guidance, then we may call our condition one in which there is a nonavailability of symbols. It would seem that there are many people today who live in such a condition, while there are others for whom the ancient symbols are still available. Between these two groups there seem to be people who are creating pseudo symbols for themselves and searching for appropriate symbols that will give them a psychic strength, a strength that can come only when one has found a meaning in life.

The Meaning of the Declaration That God Is Dead

As we have discussed above, symbols define and delimit the psychic experiences of man. In the case of the high symbol, God, the outer boundary of possible experience and of permissible ethical action was established by the content involved in the credo "I believe in God." The God symbol was usually the outer limit of the physical world also in the formal philosophical systems of the West. According to Aristotle, beyond the last orbit of the planets and stars was the abode of the Unmoved Mover. According to Karl Jaspers, the Encompassing is that which lies beyond all possible human experience. The symbol of God has stood for the ultimate, and hence it has been natural, and throughout most of history it has been appropriate, that God be spoken of in terms of the heights and of the heavenly. Just as the inverted bowl of the blue sky capped the surface of the earth, so did the conception of God at the apex of everything mundane delimit and crown the possible areas of human experience.

In the light of this understanding of the function of symbols we may observe that the philosophical meaning of the "death of God" is that the chief defining and restraining symbol of Western culture has disintegrated because it is no longer appropriate and therefore is not available to express man's sense of the limitation of his knowledge and the boundaries of his experience. This does not mean either that there is any such thing as a God apart from its epistemological function or that such an entity as God has disappeared. It may be the case that the religious meaning of the symbol God continues to function in the lives of some men but, at the same time, that such religious meaning has evaporated for others. This seems to be what the radical theologian William Hamilton has in mind when he declares that we experience God's absence today. In reference to the declaration of Thomas J. J. Altizer that there once was a God but that God really died in the event of Jesus' death, an event that has just become known to Western man through Nietzsche and the events since Nietzsche's time, we must observe that either Altizer is speaking in completely mythical terms or else he is symbolically affirming the same erosion of meaning that we have identified here as the sense content of the phrase "God is dead."

Increasing Awareness and God's Death

However, there is a deeper and more significant interpretation that can be placed upon the declaration of God's death in our day. This is a psychological understanding of the phrase. From this point of view, the announcement of God's death is a psychic awareness on the part of sensitive, religious personalities that the chief integrating symbol of Western culture no longer functions to restrain man from enacting in life his most repressed and barbaric responses and feelings. Thus, as Nietzsche declares, God being dead, all is permissible. All is permissible in human interpersonal relations because all is pure expression of raw psychic response without the restraint and delimitation of the functioning of the integrating symbol of God. The floodgates of emotion and primal-level feelings are open. The symbol God is the chief restraint on the primal or id level of experience. The function formerly performed by the symbol God was the control of the raw animal nature of man symbolized by the id. As long as that symbol functioned, the superego (or "conscience") was lively; when that symbol ceased to function, the superego collapsed.

Now that the superego has been so weakened, man's sense of identity is threatened because his ego is at the mercy of the id.

Such a condition of threat to man's personal center is experienced as extreme anxiety, and the general condition of a society made of such men is described as one of meaninglessness. Once the restraint that was built into the mind of man by the habitual usage of the limiting symbol God was relaxed, the meaning contained in and implied by that restraint was washed away. In a real way, as both Augustine and Freud have recognized, civilization is possible only by virtue of the operation of restraints upon man's psychic nature. The sociological truth of the necessity of such restraints upon human behavior for the establishment of culture has been symbolized by the conception of the social contract, the history of which is as old as Greek philosophy and as new as the call for participatory democracy by the Students for a Democratic Society.

The God symbol, as I have noted in my discussion in *The Roots of the Radical Theology*,[3] disintegrated because it was no longer able to limit the expression of raw psychic energy in the brutality of modern war. Paul Tillich clearly expressed this insight when he said that his reaction to the carnage of 1914 was to say, "God is dead." After this time the priests and ministers of institutional churches would continue to use the word "God," but it evidently was an empty usage since it had no power to restrain man from mass murder, the use of poison gas, and the use of atomic weapons. The fence that belief in God had built around the behavior of Western man was destroyed. In the nineteenth century the experience of the death of the old restraining symbols was the property of only a few, such as Marx and Nietzsche. Today that break, rupture, separation or split of alienation has fully taken place for a very great number of men in the West. For these "new ones" in Europe and America, God is dead, all moral codes are outdated, and the conceptions of patriotism and nationalism seem absurd. This psychological condition is not new, as any student of history would be quick to point out. Some of the extreme Sophists of the fifth century B.C. felt this way. The people who stormed the Bastille in the French Revolution were not completely different from those who hold today that God is dead. In every period there has arisen such a state of mind. The conditions of the eighteenth-century English rabble, reported by Charles Dickens in his novels and by Henry Fielding in *Tom Jones* (where gin replaced faith), were thoroughly modern.

In some respects those who feel the death of God as a real event in our day exhibit more religious sensitivity than we can find in the writings that have come down to us about the Sophists and the proletariat of the French Revolution and the British industrial revolution. Today the lack of any covering symbol and of any powerful restraining force upon human desire is felt, as one of the new theologians has put it, as "a pressure and a wounding." In the words of a more representative citizen: "We feel empty; kind of dead inside. We say to ourselves, Just what's the use?" This is a feeling of primordial sensitivity and a recognition of our "lostness," as well as of our brutality, to ourselves and others. The experience of the death of the God symbol is, therefore, the most important philosophical and psychological influence on the development of the new mentality.

A New Form of Consciousness

The new mentality, which recognizes that it is the loss of the major restraining symbol of Western civilization, or God, that is at the root of our social, political, philosophical, and religious crises, is akin in its irony and gentle sensibility to Socrates and his "Socratic ignorance" which knew that it knew nothing and is also a descendant of the social criticism of the Cynic school of philosophy which desired to be like Socrates. The social critic Diogenes, who lived in a tub and looked for an honest man with a lantern in the daytime, was such a Cynic.

In the first chapter I described the new mentality as a state of mind, the state of mind of persons of an active disposition who are committed to an optimistic and radical enjoyment of the world. In many respects this new state of mind is an intellectual one, respecting as it does the possibilities for significant change that technology holds, but paradoxically there is an anti-intellectualism functioning in this new form of awareness, a form of awesome fear of the very knowledge that can help man because this knowledge has been used to create weapons of mass destruction. Because of this mingled respect and fear, we are able to see in modern man's attitude toward scientific knowledge something of the fear and reverence for God that symbolized the cohesiveness of an earlier period.

This background of reverence and fear for scientific achievement forms the invisible substructure for the conscious elements that make up the new mentality.

For many decades the fact that God, the chief restraining symbol of Western culture, was losing its usefulness was an open secret among two segments of Western society, the intellectuals and the proletariat. The poor knew from experience that the symbols of love and reverence for life were not truly powerful because they did nothing to curb the exploitation of the weak and ignorant by the rich and strong. At best, religious symbols functioned to restrain the anger and revolutionary zeal of large numbers of the lower classes who were too confused to realize that Christian morality was enjoined on them but not enforced on the upper classes. Between the unemployed and the underpaid workers at the bottom of society and the intellectual who stood only a little distance from the top of society lay the great bulk of the middle class. This class, which was small in Eastern Europe, grew larger as one moved westward to Germany, France, and Great Britain.

Across the Atlantic in America the unusual configuration of society brought about by the American experiment produced a variegated middle class that in time was larger than the upper and proletarian classes taken together. In this class—until some three decades ago—the symbol God and a good many of the associated moral symbols of the Christian tradition operated with some degree of persuasion. Within this group, of course, genuine belief in the restraining symbols varied from subclass to subclass. For the most part, businessmen had no belief in these symbols beyond the pragmatic and demonstrably valid one that these symbols, if manipulated correctly, could produce attitudes and habits in the population that were good for business. The intellectuals, who were economically part of this "middle" class because of the low financial reward of teachers and of all professionals except physicians and a small number of lawyers, also were aware of the lack of real power in the religious symbols and took one of the two courses in reference to faith in God. The first course was the genuinely humane one of attempting to hide the death of God and of Christian morality from their peers by various arguments. The second course was that of militant atheism, which was never very popular and, despite the prominence of H. L. Mencken, was followed by few. Both attitudes were not genuinely responsive to the situation, of course, any more than the support of the first group by the clergy and the attack on the second group by the church and business leaders was genuinely responsive to the ills of Western society.

The Communist Party with its nineteenth-century attitude toward religion was almost identical to the second group of middle-class intellectuals and perhaps because of its unresponsive approach to the real loss of meaning in proletarian lives never made any headway in America among either the working classes or even the ill-treated groups such as the Negroes. In Latin Europe, where a nineteenth-century form of Christianity actively fought against the humanizing forces of the twentieth century, the Communist Party was more successful and built large memberships in France and Italy. In these instances neither Catholicism nor Communism really had anything vital to contribute to the problems of the people, but Communism proved to be a more progressive absolutistic nineteenth-century system than the church and hence was more successful.

Our description of the new mentality in this book generally reflects the conditions of Western society as a whole but is not presented as a complete description of the European varieties of the loss of life's meaning. The European story is much more complex than the American. In many ways the period of the death of God is older there and the resultant post-Christian man is "more advanced" than man in America. The new form of consciousness described in this book is specifically a description of the American experience, and the type of personality hinted at in these pages is the American variety of post-Christian man. This American post-Christian individual is by no means irreligous, but his religion is not the same as traditional Protestant Christianity which is still officially (despite constitutional limitations) the civic religion of the United States. The new man is not immoral, but his morality is different from the Victorian, Comstock type of Calvinistic morality that has been written into law in many states of the Union. He is not insensitive, although our first impression of him is his toughness—a toughness to be seen even in the dropout and the hippie who believes in nonviolence.

The sensitivity of this new post-Christian man is very similar to that of the sensitivity of the existentialist intellectual and churchman who fought Nazism from the underground in World War II. It is a new style of life that characterizes the new man, from the late Martin Luther King, Jr., to Eugene McCarthy to the protesting students at Berkeley. This new style of life, looked at historically, seems to be a combination of the nineteenth-century proletariat in Europe joined with the survival instinct of the twentieth-century ghetto Negro, tempered by the sensitivity of the existentialist clergy and intellectuals of our large cities. It is an improbable combination but it exists, and it has produced what the humanist of the nineteenth century so long looked for, the next development in man.

Awareness of the Cultural Rootlessness of Our Time

Basically we can say there are four psychological elements that make up the combination of sensitivity and toughness that we have called the new mentality. The first of these elements is a conscious awareness of the death of all the traditional symbols.

We have spoken of other periods and other cultural settings in which economic and social conditions have led men to experience the death of the cultural symbols which once structured and gave order and meaning to their individual and social lives. We have used as an illustration the Sophists who degenerated into cynicism after the philosophical critique of the intellectuals from Thales to the Aristotelian school. In their case all of the meaning that had been conveyed by the myths of the Olympian deities had drained away under the realities of a developing Mediterranean civilization. It was not the criticism of the philosophers but the power politics of Alexander and his successors and the demise of the city-states which killed the civic gods. In a very real way these men were aware that something had happened in their psychic lives, but it is to be doubted that they were as clear about what had happened as we can be twenty-three hundred years later.

The basic reason why ours is known as a generation for whom God is dead is that the inner workings of the human psyche are at least partially known to great masses of men. As I have noted in *The Roots of the Radical Theology*,[4] ours is a period when all education is based on a historical and evolutionary approach. This evolutionary type of thinking is the style of those who are fully living in our historical period.

The second element of the new style of thought is the tendency toward negativity and protest which exists in uneasy tension with the more positive and optimistic elements of the new thought which has great confidence in man's scientific ability. The optimism of the new mentality seems rooted in the very rational idea that what the mind of man has created, the mind of man can control. Unfortunately, life in the twentieth century has not always been rational. The irrationality of so much of our recent history has led to severely negative feelings toward a great many of our cultural institutions. Indeed, it is probably the basic feeling that man ought to be able to improve life by maturely using his rational knowledge that has led to his many exercises in protest. Men would not attempt to force improvements on a world by demonstrating if they did not believe basically in the elements that make up that world.

Unfortunately, this negativity has often been misunderstood and opposed for the wrong reasons. Under the impress of such misunderstanding the bearers of the new mentality have sometimes been driven to negate society completely by "dropping out."

"Dropping out" has had a twofold effect. The first has been good in that by retreating to a simpler form of life the bearers of the new style of thought have come closer to understanding themselves by becoming aware of the processes of life. In their dwelling upon their own experiences they have become aware of the passage of the elements of life of which they are a part. For those of less-keen awareness who desire to find a unity with the crude elements of life in a kind of biological transcendentalism, there is all too often recourse to drugs. Drugs of various kinds, in brief, open up for the less spiritually minded the vast panorama of the inner world in a fraction of the time it takes the mystical to find the bases of their own personalities by meditation and exercises. It is a dangerous thing, it would appear, to learn so much about oneself without the foregoing discipline of creed and commitment, effort and surrender. In addition, many of the drugs that are in current use have unhealthy side effects, from a lowering of the standards of moral judgment to damage to the genes of those who take them.

This attempt, by meditation and exercise on the part of some and by drug use on the part of others, to find a feeling of unity with the ever-passing elements of life is the hallmark of the third element that makes up the new mentality. This is the drive to live through a series of experiences that will lead them to maturation, that is, to a new form of growing up that will be true adulthood in the closing decades of the twentieth century. In all the bearers of the new style of thought this effort at maturation can be seen, both in the members who remain fairly stable in the activities of the old society and in the hippies and others who have deliberately dropped out.

In order to describe cogently the drive for maturation seen in the bearers of the new mentality, which we believe is the cutting edge of a society as a whole that is trying to grow up, we must list the fourth, and last, element that makes up the new mentality. This element is the recognition by the "new ones" of the split between the pure and the practical reason which has allowed man to misuse his scientific power. This recognition is, as it was for Kant at the end of the eighteenth century, a recognition of the death of the old symbols of God. Like Kant, the "new ones" see that man has devised great sources of power by the use of his intellect and has lost the psychological restraint that would have prevented him from using human knowledge destructively against human beings. This loss of restraint is a result of vast social changes in recent centuries. Therefore, the recognition of man's present spiritual plight makes all progressive people part of the "death of God" movement, but it also (for the same reasons) makes them religious men in the best sense since they are searching for new avenues to meaning in our time.

This last element also gives us a basis for understanding the most distinctive moral element of our time which is not an element of moral laxness but one of great moral concern. This is the sense of moral outrage that is the motive power behind every demonstration and protest in both the Negro and the peace movements. Such a feeling of moral outrage also explains why so many people are leaving the church, which unfortunately seems to be able to feel only the moral judgments of a distant past. It is also the reason why so many young clergymen find the *Playboy* Philosophy more religious than the teachings of their denominations. In a serious sense the *Playboy* Philosophy is a movement toward freedom and justice and is filled with a great moral outrage at the fact that Western society has operated with such hypocritical double standards for men and women and for rich and poor during many centuries. The unreflective may not recognize it, but the *Playboy* Philosophy is a kind of puritan awakening that is calling for our society to practice what it preaches—or, perhaps, to preach what it practices.

In summary, we can say that the problem of Western man which has led to the experience of the death of God is that our pretext for pretense has evaporated. Despite ourselves, we are now forced to be honest with ourselves. History—and the up-building of our knowledge—has pushed us from a life of unacknowledged bad faith to the awareness of a life of authenticity. Man has thus moved beyond himself, surpassing his symbols (of feelings felt in former days) in his newer sensitivities. Thus he has lost the utility of the older symbols which once "covered the subject" of his hopes, fears, dreams, and beliefs.

The "new ones," who include the beat, the hippies, the dropouts, and the peaceniks, have elected for authenticity, although it is a barbaric type of authenticity and deserves the name of "post-Christian." From a moral point of view we must say that it seems healthier even in its barbarity than the shallow and hypocritical Christianity it has rejected.

III

The Death
of Western Symbols

*T*ODAY we have reached the abyss of the sense of transcendence, and the new mentality is the property of an increasingly large majority of people throughout the Western world. Our era has witnessed the rise of a new theology that has rejected most of its ties with the institutional church; of a new morality that has rejected most of the moral code of the orthodox churches and of the several states; and of a new left in politics and social views that has rejected not only the old and new right, but the center, the government in power, and even the old left itself. It would seem that we were in the presence of Nietzsche's overman, who has surpassed man himself, affirming his newborn powers, living as if God were dead, relying upon himself alone.

The creative chaos of the past decade has produced a theological statement that symbolizes in emotive and social ways the philosophy of the new mentality. This theological statement is shocking; it is even absurd from a logical point of view. It is indicative of the historical roots of the new form of thought in our time that this theological statement was originally made by a revolutionary philosopher at the end of the nineteenth century, Friedrich Nietzsche. That theological statement is, of course, "God is dead." One might think that such an up-to-date generation would not express itself in nineteenth-century terms, but, as the philosopher Ludwig Wittgenstein has said, "the man who cries out with pain, or says he has pain, doesn't choose the mouth which says it."[1]

Every generation has undoubtedly considered itself the last, sacred guardians of the heritage of Western culture. Socrates is reported to have said that the younger generation of his time was utterly undisciplined—although he was later charged with having contributed to this state of affairs. Today we are not without those who see a kind of utter depravity working among those under thirty—although we would have to extend that age limit to "under forty-five" in the case of theologians and philosophers, who mature later than other groups. Those "on the fringe" or in the "outlands" are "on the boundary" in Tillich's autobiographical sense, or, perhaps, even ontologically—in Heidegger's and Jaspers' sense.

What We Learn from Fringe Groups

As we have noted above, many of the creative philosophical and theological minds of the twentieth century have concerned themselves with the fringes of society and the frontiers of knowledge. This has undoubtedly been the case because ours has been a century in which man has moved from what he previously had considered the center of civilization—at least from a standpoint of interest and respect—to a concentration of attention on the outlands, on the exotic, on the foreign and the strange. Of course every period since the Renaissance has been concerned with exploration, with the novel and the unique. The historical era we call "modern times" is coextensive with man's preoccupation with the exploration of the globe. Many satirists have made fun of the older European penchant for apes and peacocks, black pepper and silks. Alexander Pope made high fun of the people of his time because of their weaknesses for the exotic.

Indeed, a sober historian would have to recall the legends about King Solomon and the Queen of Sheba almost three thousand years ago that show us a time that loved the new and strange as much as ours. The ancient Greeks and Romans shared this enthusiasm too, and the gladiatorial games with their African beasts pitted against barbarians stand as a monument to the jaded appetites produced by continuous exposure to the novel. Luke said of the Athenians of this period that they spent their time listening to and discussing something new every day (Acts 17:21).

What makes our period any different from these earlier times? In what way is the interest shown by us in the marginal, the peripheral, unique in the history of man? It is precisely because the interest of the mid-twentieth century is not solely on that which is exterior to Western culture but, for almost the first time in history, *attention has been turned with great intensity on the peripheral and shadowy aspects of our own society.* It is true that many of the bearers of the new mentality parade themselves in clothing that reminds us of Marco Polo returning from Cathay, or of the garb affected by sailors returning from whaling expeditions. Many of those who have become hippies or who wish to be known as hippies do dress in East Indian garb, or like stevedores or in the rags worn by the returning Confederate soldiers at the end of *Gone with the Wind.* On the surface, it would seem that here is a generation like any other, with a childish love of the unusual and a youthful, unphilosophical eclecticism. Why would this judgment not hold true?

The surface judgment made above is not true simply because the elements and motives that form the thought world that we call the new mentality are not primarily elements of attraction to the exotic, nor are they motives of titillation and jaded sensibilities. Rather, the elements that make up the new mentality— and specifically the elements that reveal to us the dissolution of the symbolic foundations of Western culture—are precisely a sense of moral outrage on the part of the alienated over the prostitution of the ideals and knowledge that are foundational to our culture. It is not because those who sense the death of God are irreligious or uncaring that they declare that life is meaningless as it is presently lived; it is because they are shocked and bewildered at the apparent desire of people to live meaningless lives that they frankly say that our culture has died. Paul Goodman somewhere has said that our culture has the powers and pleasures of a race of aristocrats but has the morale of a race of slaves. It is the apprehension of the meaningless formality of religion, at best, and the damnably harmful teachings of the churches in favor of the *status quo* that have driven so many of the sensitive and feeling persons of today out of the church and some into an outright declaration of the death of God.

Motives Behind the Death of Traditional Symbols

The motives that have produced the abyss of any sense of supranatural transcendence and have made possible (although not yet actual) only an immanent experience of transcendence can basically be grouped under three headings.

1. There are motives arising from the recognition that much of institutional religion and the civic morality of middle-class America is the enemy of life itself. Motives that can be subsumed under this general heading I will call *vitalistic motives*.

Basic apprehensions on the part of those who bear the new mentality that can be included in this vitalistic revolt against present-day religion would also include the rejection of the literalism that is characteristic not only of fundamentalists but, in a more sophisticated fashion, of theologians and ministers and many laymen of all denominations. People of the new mentality cannot understand the lack of imagination of those who are not aware of man's capacity to respond to myths and symbols. They reject the lack of sensitivity on the part of so many religious and moral people to the inner meaning of religious symbols and to the basic purpose of moral insights. The alienated look in horror at the sacrifice of moral purposes by those who insist on the letter of the law and at the utter lack of concern for a genuine religious response by those who insist on certain creedal formulas and ritual devotions. For this reason many members of the new thought form prefer eclectic rituals loosely based on Hinduism and Zen. Many others have an increasing respect for the unsophisticated but deeply emotional devotions of the Negro churches and of the unusual spiritualistic sects.

A very deep part of the motivation for rejection of society by the "hip" is the unthinking willingness of the masses of Americans to support any kind of war that may come along. The reaction against the Vietnam war is, as Thomas J. J. Altizer once told this writer, a very real part of the experience of the death of God. The bearers of the new mentality have responded affirmatively to the deeply religious meaning of the "Ban the Bomb" symbol devised by the peace movement, headed by the agnostic philosopher Bertrand Russell.[2] These "new ones" have also responded to the basic meaning of Albert Schweitzer's call for man to practice reverence for life. The alienated of today have become more and more sure that modern society in the West—and increasingly in the East, due to the development of atomic weapons in Communist China—is rapidly being forced out of a stance where many options as to future action are possible and into a position where the future is painted in stark contrast between two opposing lines of conduct: peace or war. This is also due to the fact that television and radio have enabled the average man to develop a broader political awareness. Raw information comes straight to us, undigested.

The traditionally described ethical position of "grayness" between several positions, all involving both good and evil, is no longer tenable. On the one side lie the dangers of allegiance to nonviolence and peace; on the other side, the dangers of espousing a violent philosophy and thus bringing closer the day of nuclear war. The humorous contrast of flower power and police power, seen in some recent civil disturbances, puts the issue in sharp focus. The new mentality recognizes this contrast and makes its decision, for good or ill, for peace over war. There is no longer a position that honestly asks for justice rather than for love. It is clear now that it is a matter of either love or death.

2. The second general heading under which we may group the motives that underlie the experience of the death of God

among the members of the fringe groups who bear the new mentality are those motives and apprehensions we may call *reactions against the spiritual values of main-line Western culture*. The first of these rejections, and perhaps the most important, is the rejection by the "new ones" of the insensitivity of so much of main-line religious and ethical thought to an awareness of the ongoing processes of life. The future-oriented, pleasure-deferring basis of Protestant morality and middle-class petty capitalism is the major bone of contention between those who consider themselves "turned on" or "cool" and the respectable ones. The bearers of the new mentality believe that the spirits of those who cannot enjoy the present moment must be dead. Psychologically the difference is between a psyche that is free of unneeded restraint and a psyche that is unhealthily repressed and negated by fears that bear little relation to the real world. In brief, the new ones have found something of that inner freedom which the higher religions have always promised to man. The problem seems to be one of determining whether or not the freedom of the new ones has not gone so far as to also have jettisoned some essential restraining elements which may cause discontent in man but which also make civilization possible. An interesting discussion of the cool ones and their rejection of traditional spiritual outlooks is given by Henry W. Malcolm in *Never Trust a God Over Thirty*.[3]

Another element in the motivation of the new ones' rejection of traditional spiritual outlooks is the commitment of the bearers of the new mentality to the necessity and positivity of change. Philosophically and theologically, a great element in Western philosophical thought has been the immutability of God, that is, the unchangeability of God. For twenty-four hundred years Western philosophical thought has been dominated by the conception of the unchanging deity, the Unmoved Mover of Aristotle. Although Christianity has always stressed the livingness of God, it is significant that Christianity adopted the philosophy of Aristotle for the basis of its theological system—as seen in Thomas Aquinas—and has always stressed

"the Father of lights with whom there is no variation or shadow
due to change" (James 1:17).

Of course, the theologians intended, probably quite rightly,
to stress the constancy and faithfulness of God, while Aristotle
intended to stress the static view of the universe held by the
physicists of his time. Unfortunately, the Christian tradition drew
the conclusion from the unchangeableness of God that there
was something good and holy about the old, the proven, the
changeless, and therefore sanctified the traditional. In this
idolatry of the past and the finished, Christian theology followed the lead of Plato, who taught the illusory and valueless
nature of the temporal, changing world and attributed reality
and worth only to the invisible and unchanging abstract world
of ideas. To this day much of traditional Christianity is resistant
to social and ideological change when it is not outrightly hostile
to it. It is this fixation on tradition that is rejected by the new
mentality. The new ones believe that we should rest content in
change. Heraclitus rather than Plato must be our example. We
must recognize reality for what it is: one change after another.
We must learn to embrace life as it actually is, a flux of ever-
new proportions and configurations; not attempt to create an
unreal world where the answers to every question have already
been given and where the best way to live tomorrow was thought
about centuries ago. We must learn to live relatively with relativity.

The new mentality also stresses man's need to accept the
ambiguity of life. Man must give up his neurotic desire for absolute certainty in affairs of the human spirit. The drive for precise statement and detailed direction must be limited to the
sciences and not mistakenly fastened on to man.

This emphasis upon the need for sensitivity to the weaknesses
of mankind, which can often be seen as man's greatest strength,
is a decisive and creative offering of the new mentality to the
life of man. The emphasis upon conformity in behavior and
upon efficiency in work habits which may have been necessary
in the disciplining of workers coming fresh from the fields to

the factories of the early industrial revolution and which created the army of workers in which Karl Marx reposed such confidence has resulted in a barren, almost cultureless, citizenry in all the Western countries, including the Communist bloc. It is interesting to note that the first sign of the awakening of the new mentality is an increase in interest and creativity and the stimulation of the imagination. This is not to say that there is a complete lack of imagination or a lack of interest in experiment and creativity among the vast middle classes which stretch from semiskilled workers to judges and physicians. It is to say—what has been remarked on many occasions—that even the imagination of so much of the stable classes is exercised in a kind of lockstep conformity that keeps the individual from rising to a point where he can criticize himself and his own class.

This absolutism of one's own beliefs and security shows the failure of the middle classes to rise to a position where they are capable of recognizing the ambiguities of life: physical, moral, and economic. In extreme cases this failure to recognize ambiguity results in the moralistic attitude of those who seek to ban every book they do not understand and expresses itself politically in the naïve identification of their country's foreign and domestic policy with the will of God.

Rigid types of personalities, which are endemic in our mainline society, are so psychologically threatened by any kind of ambiguity that they must for their own health's sake find the artificial securities provided by dogmas of both church and state. It is thus clear that the new mentality, which not only accepts but rejoices in the ambiguities of life—in those hidden and mysterious workings of the processes of nature and of the poetic and irrational elements which make up the sphere of human activity in both the personal and the social areas—is disturbing to many members of our society. Until all men learn to live comfortably with change and to find joy rather than fear in the ambiguities and mysteries of human existence, it appears that the only free spirits on earth will be those who have rejected institutional religion and the doctrines of political and social cohesiveness.

3. The third heading upon which we may group the motives that underlie the experiences on the part of the "new ones" that have led them to announce that the God of Western culture is dead may be called the *societal motives*. These social apprehensions are of three major subtypes: (*a*) Those motives which arise from the insights into social psychology that are a common experience among persons who bear the new mentality. The thrust of these insights is that the doctrinaire emphasis upon individualism in America and among capitalists throughout the world is demonic and simply incorrect as a description of how true individuality is achieved. (*b*) The sense of moral outrage which is the strongest psychological force in all thinking members of our society from the least educated to the university professor. This moral outrage is directed toward the dysfunctional policies of American government at home and abroad and the resultant loss of life in war and loss of domestic social unity in rioting and race hatred. The new mentality is clearly marked by this sense of moral outrage in both the activist members of the new thought form who struggle against main-line society's programs and in the passive members of the new group who drop out in frustration and despair. (*c*) The optimistically liberal, almost religious, belief in the perfectibility of man that leads the new ones to believe that racial problems can be settled, that peace can be achieved in the cold and hot wars and in the tendency to practice habits of self-fulfillment that are implicitly believed to lead to human happiness.

The Shape of Radical Theology

Growing out of the three basic motives that have led to the rejection of traditional religious and political views with their idealistic forms of transcendent thought is the philosophy of the new mentality, a theology of man, now known as radical theology.

Radical theology is the heir to a long line of philosophical and theological reflection and speculation which now embodies the psychological insight of Freud, the awareness of the function of symbol of Jung, the operation of dialectic in thought and history of Hegel, and the moral and social outrage of Karl Marx. This radical theology is proclaimed with the passionate intensity of an existentialistic approach to life by young professors of religion and philosophy and by campus chaplains all over America. In a real way the new or radical theology is the emotional or feeling base for the entire structure of the new mentality, as it contains the primitive Christian sense of saving purpose, the existentialist feeling that the meaning of life revolves around the responsible individual, and the Marxist denunciation of economic and national oppression. This may sound like a unique synthesis of unusual elements, but basically each revolves around a keen moral sense and a feeling of personal responsibility. It is in this morally responsible way that the various elements that go to make up the new theology are brought together and crystallized into a radically new way of looking at the world. If anyone doubts that such a mixture is possible, he needs only to examine the life and teaching of a successful campus chaplain, or the utterances of student protest leaders.

The Rise of Radical Theology[4]

The literature covering the new or radical theology that is sensitive to the split in modern man's self-consciousness and of the death of the restraining and integrating symbols of our time has reached large proportions. I have already discussed the historical roots of this movement in a thorough study,[5] so we will only briefly review the forces that brought this theological style into prominence in the 1960's.

First, the new theology is the heir of the contrapuntal tradition in the West that has brought forward the negative element of the historical dialectic from the time of Thales and Socrates to the radical socialist and sectarian leaders of the twentieth century. This element has consistently survived disapproval, repression, and even persecution, offering a creative no to the yes of conformity and thoughtlessness from the time of the Greeks to the administration of Johnson. Some of its major figures, who later have been called heroes, are Socrates, Jesus, Luther, Comte, Feuerbach, Nietzsche, Kierkegaard, Marx, Freud, and Schweitzer. An investigation of the genuine messages of these men in the context of their own historical situations makes it an obvious insight that the great critics have been the truly constructive personalities in the progress of Western culture.

The more immediate background of the radical theology is the rise of the problem of the separation of faith and reason in the Enlightenment and the philosophical separation of the pure reason—or scientific reason—from the practical (or religious and moral) reason in the foundational philosophy of Immanuel Kant. Kant related them to each other, but the Kantian synthesis of the pure and the practical reason dissolved under the crises and scientific developments of the eighteenth and nineteenth centuries. This separation of the pure and practical reason, without a workable mediating principle between them, became the intellectual inheritance of the late nineteenth and twentieth centuries. Men worked to strengthen one or the other side of this dichotomy: some emphasized emotion; others, tough-minded thought. In the midst of this fundamental intellectual struggle, the liberal tradition in theology, stemming from Schleiermacher and emphasizing the psychological feeling of dependence on the universe on the part of man, surpassed the orthodox theological stream—which became increasingly non-creative—and in many instances hardened into the anti-intellectual position now called fundamentalism. I have called the eighteenth and nineteenth centuries in theology a period of "critical scholarship and rationalistic orthodoxy," trying to synthesize the four major elements that made up the liberal tradition in this period, which elements gradually brought about the absolute polarization of Christian thinkers and believers in genneral into two schools. These schools still exist in a general way in the twentieth century, and the extremes of the two positions are called "fundamentalist" and "modernist." Of course, in the twentieth century, the largest number of thinkers, clergy and churchmen at large, would fall between the extremes represented by these two groups.

Major Elements of Liberal Theology

The four major elements of the liberal tradition in theology and the reactions to it on the part of the conservative or orthodox theologians and believers, which formed an immediate intellectual background for the rise of the new theology, were:

1. The rise of modern Biblical scholarship, and the consequent change of place of the Bible in Western thought.

The development of literary techniques for the interpretation and understanding of the Biblical text, joined to the development of scientific methods for the study of the historical, archaeological, and cultural setting and background of the Bible, obviously forms one of the feet upon which the new theology, as an outgrowth of the older liberal theology, stands. It is quite true, of course, that the use of "higher" and "lower" criticism of the Bible has been accepted for many years by the mainstream of Protestantism and by the intellectual elements within the Roman Catholic Church as well as by the reform wing of Judaism. In the use of linguistic, historical, archaeological, and even philosophical tools of interpretation and understanding of the Bible, there is little difference between neo-orthodox Presbyterians, Methodists, Lutherans, and other Protestants, and the Bible scholars (at least for the last ten years) in Roman Catholic universities and Rabbinical scholars in Jewish seminaries.

In the wealth of helpful information and the usefulness of the more advanced methods of interpretation such as "form criticism," "demythologization," and the constantly evolving methods of literary study of the Bible, there is little debate between a very large middle segment of the clergy and the religious scholars of every faith. However, the whole question of modern Biblical scholarship is much at issue among a growing segment of the religious community in America, that community of thought which considers itself the true heir of primitive Christianity and the guardian of the orthodox faith, which can best be entitled the "Right-Wing Church in America."[6] Since the sociological description of this church movement has often been discussed elsewhere and since I have discussed it in *Radical Christianity and Its Sources,* as well as in articles,[7] I will limit myself here to say that this is the type of "Christian thought" which equates true belief with an uncritical acceptance of the literal text of the Bible as long as the interpretation of the Bible is made in accordance with its economic, social, racial, and political ideals—which are usually those of the white, property-owning middle class.

It is interesting to note that the shrillest denunciations of the new theology have come from sources which hold views of the Bible that refuse to accept the findings of modern Bible scholarship. Indeed, many of these right-wing radical critiques tend to lump together liberals, neo-orthodox, and "death of God" theologians, claiming not to be able to distinguish one from the other.

2. The rise of the "history of religions" school, in which the beliefs of the Bible were identified as related to other religions both primitive and modern.

The rise of scholarly interest in the connection of Christianity not only with its parent religion, Biblical Judaism, but with Islam, a sister religion, and with Buddhism, Hinduism, Shintoism, and the several religions of China has been one of the most interesting occurrences in theological history. The effort to discover what the historians of religion had learned about the religions of the world and how this new knowledge might assist Christian theology seems to be one of the most promising movements in theology today. During the last three years of his life, the late Paul Tillich, one of the most creative theological minds in history, was attempting to relate the disciplines of systematic theology and the history of religions to each other, hoping to find a way to revitalize Christian theology on the one hand and to help settle some of the great problems of the world on the other.[8]

Although members of the middle-of-the-road theological positions have welcomed the insights into other religions brought into being by the investigations and reflections of the historians of religion, the extreme right wing has been unwilling to accept much of this material beyond what it has found useful in foreign mission work. The conservative mind has been happy to utilize both this kind of knowledge and also that made available by anthropology in order to devise ways to convert members of other religions, but it has not been willing to learn anything spiritual from these other faiths that might improve their version of or understanding of Christianity.

3. The struggle between the fundamentalists (or Bible literalists) and the promoters of the theory of evolution.

This struggle was played out in the nineteenth century in Europe, but has continued into the mid-twentieth century in the United States. It was essentially settled in favor of the evolutionists by 1930, but it is a continuing source of friction in various strata of American society. The fundamentalists, who make up a very large number of persons in the United States, have never admitted that they lost the struggle and consider the argument still open. Even in main-line denominations there occasionally arises a problem in this respect with a Sunday school teacher being dismissed for "teaching evolution" and a controversy in the congregation taking shape. It is fairly obvious that the kinds of mentality that have not been able to grasp the structure of sixth-grade science would be vehement enemies of radical theologians who declare that ours is the time of the death of God.

4. The quest, from the very beginning of the modern (liberal) study of the Bible, for the essential facts about Jesus of Nazareth. (This quest for "the historical Jesus" as distinct from "the Christ of faith" ultimately failed. The content of liberal, "Jesus-centered" piety evaporated under the heat of critical scholarship.)

The period of the first quest for the historical Jesus came to an end with the analysis of the movement's failure by Albert Schweitzer in his famous work *Von Reimarus zu Wrede: Eine Geschichte der Leben-Jesu-Forschung.*[9] Schweitzer's famous study was made in 1906 and translated into English in 1910. We may see his work as the signal of the death of the liberal critical scholarship that undergirded liberal Christianity in the nineteenth century. Eight years later, in 1914, the horrors of modern warfare signaled the death of the liberal ethical optimism that was the driving force of religion and Western culture in the Victorian era and in that happy period between the Boer War and World War I. It was over thirty-five years (after 1945) from the date of the English translation of *The Quest of the Historical Jesus*[10] before German and American scholars became interested in pursuing a new quest for the historical Jesus. The "new quest" is still going on but has apparently not attracted the attention and support that the old quest did, and is apparently the interest of only a few New Testament scholars and even fewer systematic theologians who are looking for a fruitful direction in which to move because of the current impasse between the right-wing and left-wing followers of Bultmann. This struggle in the Bultmannian camp is a long story which we will not take up here, but essentially it involves the question of whether "the new being," or existential salvation, which Bultmann feels is the essence of the New Testament, requires there having been a real Jesus in whom this new being was manifested, or whether such an existential salvation is not available apart from the actual existence of such a person.

Of course for the fundamentalists and the very conservative type of believer, considerations such as the above are as remote as the far side of the moon. For in this tradition the Biblical record is simply accepted and a great deal of attention is paid to Biblical archaeology, the findings of which are used to "prove" what is already believed. This tradition often involves a great deal of attention to scholarship in the sense of amassing information and mastering details. Great attention is paid to the geography of Israel and the Near East and to studies of Biblical chronology. There really has never been a problem about the historical Jesus for this mentality since the critical spirit of scholarship is not part of its makeup.

The Future of This Radical Theology

While no one can completely predict the future of any movement of thought, some indicators do exist that seem to point toward some definite areas of activity in the future developments of radical theology. These indicators include the interests of the participants in the various radical movements in America, the influence of certain ideologists, and the challenges posed by the crises through which America—and religion in general—is now passing.

Basically, we can look forward to a deepening and widening of the philosophical base of the radical theology as the new mentality (of which it is a part) continues to mature. The young people who take part in the Radical Education Project[11] and who read *Ramparts*[12]—responding positively to their messages of the need for social change—will go on to take places of power in America's social structure.

These young people have rejected most—if, indeed, not all— of their ties with the institutional churches, but have by no means lost their interest in religion. To the contrary, many of the young radicals are vitally interested in religion—although their interest is in the fundamental sensitivities of men toward the needs and hopes of their inner selves and of all other men. Additionally, many young radicals, including the hippies (although this is not limited to them), are fascinated by the Oriental religions. The adornment of their persons with beads (as in Hindu India), the wearing of Nehru shirts, the popularity of gurus and Hindu sages among musical groups and on college campuses, all attest to this fact.

The young radicals, then, are not religionless people. I would venture to say that the current generation under thirty years of age are more interested in religion than any such generation in the twentieth century. By the same reasoning, although this generation of radicals have loudly (and sincerely) rejected the traditional moral codes of the civil law and the main-line churches, they are not, for that reason, immoral or unmoral. Rather, their morality is of a different order, on a different plane or dimension, from that of their elders whose morality is piously mouthed.

The New Morality

The "new morality" that characterizes the young radicals of today is essentially a morality of universal love. It is not a morality that grows out of a reasoned ethical system based on enlightened self-interest (as in modern business ethics), or on projections of which activities will lead to the greatest good for the greatest number (as in civil law and institutionalized forms of utilitarian ethics, seen in some economic doctrinal systems), but is (to the utter fright of many churchmen) based more on the love ethic of the Jesus of the Gospels and the compassion of the Buddha taught in some Buddhist sects, such as the Pure Land sect of Buddhism in Japan.

Under the influence of centuries of Christian and Jewish teaching (plus the growing knowledge of Hindu and Buddhist teaching since the nineteenth century) the modern mentality has evolved to a higher "pitch" and wider dimension of ethical sensitivity. This "pitch" or "tone" of sensitivity has advanced or "risen" to such a degree that it has made the "leap" (or transition) from accumulated quantity to that of a new quality—or a uniquely ethical cast of mind.

The content of this new ethical state of consciousness is simple and direct: the Golden Rule of all the higher religions— "Do unto others as you would have them do unto you" . . . (as well as in Schweitzer's reverence for life), and thus it is inner-directed ("unto you") and outer-directed ("do unto others") at one and the same time.

The new ethical sensitivity thus transcends (as Jesus, the

prophets, Confucius, and the Bhagavad-Gita's authors always have transcended) the philosophical problem of the one and the many, the individual and the group.

And this new mentality in ethics has transcended even the most sensitive of the old teachers (including Tillich) because it has moved beyond the courage of doubt into the leap ("risk"?) of affirmation. One might call the content of this transcendental unity of affirmation *the reverence for life of a new morality of life itself*—although it can, and probably must, be described in purely empirical, naturalistic terms.

A radically new theology of universal love and a radically new morality of reverence for life—all life—would be expected to usher in new and radical social and political views as well. In this the new movements of youth from the hippies to the Students for a Democratic Society do not disappoint us. Those who are participating in the new mentality definitely share a unique social consciousness and many of them go on to express this consciousness in political form.

The Radical Type

Basically, the radical movement in America is made up of persons under thirty years of age—especially those in the two subgroups of this age group who have (1) either been matriculated at a college or university, or (2) have had their origin in one of the deprived areas of the nation, such as an urban ghetto, or a poverty pocket in the rural South, and who have been influenced by one of the civil rights or peace movement organizations. However, we will be wrong, as the press is often wrong, if we think of the new mentality as being found solely among the young. There are many members of, or sympathizers with, radical groups, directly or indirectly in sympathy with their aims, who are over thirty.

Earlier in this book we made reference to the fact that many theologians and clergymen share this vision and perhaps a majority of them are over thirty, due to the length of their professional training. For the same reason, many other members of the academic profession who are over thirty share in the new mentality and support radical social and political groups. The Radical Education Project, headquartered at Ann Arbor, Michigan, and affiliated with S.D.S., is a kind of clearinghouse for literature and speakers for those in the university world who are interested in a radical approach to the solution of current social and political ills and willing to run the risk of identifying themselves with S.D.S. The radicality of this group, which might be taken as characteristic of the political feeling of those who share the new mentality, is increasingly being attacked in recent years as being Communistic, although this is more of a general rather than a specific charge. Even governmental officials have called S.D.S. a Communist-front organization. This charge must be seriously investigated, for it sounds unlikely because the type of individuals who make up the new radical organizations and who have been named the "new left" are emotionally and philosophically opposed to the principles of Communism as that political system is preached and practiced by any present or past governmental regime in Europe, Cuba, or Asia. A possible basis on which such charges are made is the fact that the members of the new left are not anti-Communistic and that they are willing to speak with, debate with, and even accept an occasional point from those who are avowedly Trotskyites or Communists. Many of the meetings of radical political groups do have some Communists in attendance. Because of this openness and willingness to talk with leftists the extreme conservatives brand the young radicals as Communists or Communist dupes. In another vein there is in the United States a fractionally small Communist youth group whose members occasionally associate with the new left, as well as there being extremely tiny groups of pro-Chinese Communist supporters and pro-Castroites and Trotskyites. The pro-Chinese group is contained in the miniscule youth league of the Progressive Labor Party, which is a part of the old left and not of the new left.

The new left in politics, which expresses the sentiments of

those bearing the new mentality, would seem to be psychologically immune to Communism, for it is against all systems of law and order that deemphasize the individual and that put property rights or national rights or states' rights above the absolute freedom of development of the individual. In no joking sense we can say that the new mentality's bearers would make even worse Communists than they make Democrats or Republicans. Since they find the *status quo* in this country with so many freedoms utterly rigid and desire to change it in an almost anarchic way, one can imagine their reaction to the strict controls of the Communist Party and a Communist state. Perhaps no ideological group despises and even fears the new radicals so much as the Communists. Any extreme, rigid type of personality or political system hates and fears the truly free individual. The persons who call the new left and the hippies "Communists" may be right in thinking them dangers to the *status quo,* while being inaccurate in their political evaluation. The events of Chicago in August, 1968, may even indicate that S.D.S. and the new left are really to the "left" of Communism.

Marxism and the New Left

We cannot leave this discussion of the new left without honestly expressing the deep affinities the new left has to what we might call the radical morality of early Marxism. Basically, Karl Marx was a social prophet who denounced injustice, oppression and exploitation in a manner not only similar to, but directly influenced by, the teachings of the Hebrew prophets, of Jesus, and of the early Christian church. Although Marx considered himself the enemy of religion and unfortunately saddled his movement with a broad streak of antireligion that confused the religious impulse with the perversion of it in the institutional churches, he actually articulated the social morality of the Judeo-Christian religion. The new left responds to this ethical sensitivity in Marx just as older radicals in the religious and academic communities have done in the past and are doing now. The new left does read Marx. It is perhaps not snide to say that if those who undoubtedly equate reading Marx with being a Communist would only read some Marx (beyond the *Communist Manifesto*), they might see that most Communists are not Marxists, and that many people who are not Communists are Marxists (as are the Socialists of West Germany), and that it might be possible to learn something from one of the keenest minds of the nineteenth century.

There are two other reasons why the new left is so frequently identified with Communism. The first is that the new left is honestly and openly a movement for radical social change. It is a shame, but it is still true, that apparently a large majority of Americans cannot tell one kind of movement for social change from another. The masses of our citizens are unable to tell a member of the NAACP from a Communist agent (such identifications are often made, especially in the Deep South) because of simple ignorance of anything political or philosophical. Eventually, perhaps, the American people will learn the kind of truth about our internal life that our State Department has had to learn about our relations with other countries: that democratic social change, as radical as is needed to overcome injustice and need, is the only antidote to eventual—although unnecessary and fruitless—communist revolution which feeds on the injustice of other forms of government and will break out where the rights of people are forever thwarted by anticommunist governments. This lesson from overseas, if learned well and put into operation, might save us from an internal war in our urban ghettos.

In all events the new left, the political arm of the new mentality, is committed to and is actively working for radical social change.

The second reason the new left has given some foundations to the charges of Communist influence is the radicals' openness to talk to Communists (and to anyone else who will talk), which we have mentioned above. Perhaps there is a bit more than this to it, as Jack Newfield has remarked in *A Prophetic Minority,* for the members of the new left simply do not have the inborn (although they were actually instilled and not really inborn) prejudices against Communism of those thirty-five and over who remember Korea and the Berlin Crisis. Perhaps the events of the Soviet and Warsaw Pact powers' invasion of Czechoslovakia and Russia's warlike threats to West Germany may bring a more reasonable assessment of Communism to the fore among the young of the new left.

The rise of the "yippies," or politically activistic hippies, to national attention and their national nuisance value during the Presidential campaigns and elections have made many people believe that the new leftists really are Communists. Sad to relate, in a great number of cases, these extreme left-wing individuals are more dangerous to a society than the Communists. In fact, the S.D.S. movement pretty much stays away from yippie gatherings. The yippies are a kind of *reductio ad absurdum* of radicality—an anarchy of the absurd.

Future Development of Radical Religion

Thomas Luckmann, in *The Invisible Religion*,[13] writes of the development of a new social religion that has actually already become the heir of church and synagogue in industrialized societies. This set of symbols is the "modern sacred cosmos," and it is basically in charge even in the churches (which it has hollowed out and filled with its own content). Its symbols of "ultimate concern" all center on the private sphere, and stress the dignity of individualism and self-autonomy (while leaving control of the primary social institutions such as government and business alone). This new, social religion stresses self-discovery and self-realization—shades of Huxley's *soma!* In this "symbolic universe" there is an emphasis placed on the family as an extension of the private sphere and a granting of more freedom in sexual conduct—as these activities do not concern and do not threaten the primary and powerful social institutions.[14]

The new or radical theology held by those who have been

moved by the teaching of the "death of God" theologians and whose political views are expressed by groups like S.D.S. is the mortal enemy of this invisible, civic religion.

A Movement Against the Civic Religion

Radical theology is perhaps more of a protest against the civic religion practiced in America than against the traditional dogmas of the institutional churches. This insight comes from many discussions with radical thinkers, who insist that they like their church theologians to express the kind of conservative views found in *Christianity Today* and who insist that the "death of God" experience must be linked to the opposition to Vietnam and support for civil rights. Considering these circumstances and attitudes, it grows increasingly clear that the radical theology is different in content (in many respects) as well as different in concerns from the traditional Protestant and Catholic versions of Christianity. The older liberalism and conservatism differed in degrees of emphasis of doctrines, but chiefly differed in concerns. Such a comparison between main-line Christian denominations and the radical movement with respect to doctrines and belief does not seem useful. It is not that their emphases differ, but that their outlooks are opposed. What one affirms, the other denies. Such is the meaning of the word "radical" today when used to modify theology.

Paradoxes, Enigmas, and Contradictions

Although traditional (i.e., Protestant neo-orthodoxy in the last few decades) theology and radical theology negate each other, paradoxically, many people within the churches are moving consciously or unconsciously toward a radical religious stance. Like the slight variations of color within a bird species, church members begin at one end of the scale and shift, shade by shade, toward a totally new color on the opposite end of the spectrum. No denomination (as distinct from a sect) contains birds of all one shade. Each denomination is a mixed flock of birds running from a deep blue color to bright red. How can we account for this situation, apart from the fact that individuals react as total men to the problems of their times, and not as "Methodists" or "Lutherans"? Is the tolerance or sensitivity level of these individual Christians the major factor in the increasing similarity of response between conservative Methodists and Presbyterians (for example), on the one side, and liberal and/or "radical" Methodists and Presbyterians, on the other? I believe that this sensitivity level is the chief factor here, a sensitivity that responds to the stresses and questions of secular society (including church politics!) in the only way possible for the individuals involved. Why do I say the only way possible? Because the traditional symbols (doctrines, rites, customs, traditions) have been hollowed out from within by a rapid decay in belief. The reasons for this decay of belief are so complex that I can only refer the reader to my previous books on the subject, *The Roots of the Radical Theology* and *Radical Christianity and Its Sources.* Essentially, the rise of a form of historic self-consciousness and an increasing reliance upon the scientific method has undercut belief in God's providence, as well as in his creation and continuing governance of the world.

The vacuum that has been created within the churches by the hollowing out of the traditional belief system has not been tolerable, because even for those who do not attend a church, the values represented by the traditional symbols were important as keys to the understanding of the meaning of life and the ordering of society (for example, the function of the symbol "God" in law). The vacuum that has been growing increasingly stronger in the awareness of man in the twentieth century has consequently been filled by new content that represents feelings that have their origins outside the traditional boundaries of the church and its historical concern. The basic question that has been implicit in this refilling of the older symbols has been, How do we find "grace" in this world? Of course, for most people this question has been unconscious, for it would not occur to them consciously to look for resources of the spirit within the finite life of the existing world. For some theologians, however, an explicit question has been raised, How is culture a source for theology? The works of the religious naturalists, many of whom follow the ideas formulated about God and the world by Alfred North Whitehead, are rather specifically directed to this question. Representatives of this tradition are Bernard E. Meland, B. M. Loomer, both of the older Chicago School of Theology, and Henry Nelson Wieman, as well as the philosopher, Charles Hartshorne.[15]

Most theologians, however, have not approached the doctrinal vacuum in this way. Rather, they have responded to the crisis in theology in the twentieth century by way of the program of liberalism which consists in emphasizing certain concerns and doctrines at the expense of others, or by way of neo-orthodoxy which chiefly consists of a social interpretation of the Bible's call for individual and group righteousness. In a very real way the sensitive reinterpretation of Christianity as a movement of concern to heal the divisions among men and to assist in the solution of the problems of race, poverty, and war is the last motion and finest expression of the neo-orthodox movement in America. This movement, although now passing from the scene, has recently found new life and is revitalizing many of the main-line denominations.

One might well ask, under these circumstances, why neo-orthodoxy needs to be surpassed (and/or replaced) as a theological stance? The answer to this question has not been difficult to give: Neo-orthodoxy has not prevented the drastic breakdown of cultural elements in American society although it has honestly warned of the threat of such a breakdown for thirty years. Neo-orthodoxy is dying because its greatest representatives (such as the several editors of *The Christian Century* and *Christianity and Crisis*) see nothing but the abyss of race war before us. Again and again, the neo-orthodox speak out in pessimistic terms. This movement of negativity can never provide the "push" needed to meet our common problems, while the optimism of radical theology can.

The radical theology we see as leading us positively toward a difficult future constitutes a new interpretation of the "sacral order" (i.e., of "the things of the Spirit"). The basic insight lying beneath the new approach to sacred symbols is this: Religion is about man and his needs. In the words of many "new Christians," "To be a Christian means to try to help men in their needs." Fundamentally, the symbols of the new Christianity (i.e., radical or new theology) are the partly conscious, but chiefly unconscious, results of a culturewide substitution of anthropology for theology. The radicals of today feel, in most instances, that the old content of religious symbols had the same thrust. At least this is the major insight of Paul van Buren in *The Secular Meaning of the Gospel,* of William Hamilton in *The New Essence of Christianity,* and of Richard L. Rubenstein in *The Religious Imagination.*[16] This vision of theology as (at least partly) anthropology was first given systematic expression by Ludwig Feuerbach in the nineteenth century. Feuerbach is largely unknown, except to some philosophers and theologians, although it is often remarked that Feuerbach influenced Karl Marx. The radicals know Feuerbach—although only William Hamilton makes a close connection with Feuerbach's thought. Hamilton deliberately named his book *The New Essence of Christianity* after Feuerbach's *The Essence of Christianity.*[17]

Feuerbach's importance for our time lies in the remarkable positive religious principle he laid down in his "religious humanism." He anticipated the position of much of radical Christianity when he adopted this thesis from Hegel's early theological writings: "God is love, and love is God. . . . There is no other Divinity than love. . . . Religion is the same as love."[18] This principle is positive and optimistic, and it is humanistic. It is in agreement with the declaration of Paul Goodman, who said: "With the increasing powerlessness of persons and the ordering of their behavior by systems of technology, the religion problem is not now how to save souls, but how to have human beings at all."[19]

And this principle rests on the basic assumption of the modern or new mentality, that the supernatural gods are no more. Man is the proper object of man's search for transcendence. If there is "God" in the universe, we can know him only through man. In Nietzsche's words about the old God of the supranatural order, "God is dead."

IV

The Post-New Morality

*U*NDER the influence of centuries of Christian and Jewish teaching, plus millennia of Hindu-Buddhist teaching, the modern mentality has evolved to a higher dimension of ethical sensitivity than ever before. The "pitch" or direction upward of this ethical sensitivity is visibly and even measurably increasing from year to year in the countries of Western Europe, North America, and of Japan and other heavily Westernized countries. The reasons for this significant growth in moral sensitivity include the use of atomic weapons at the end of World War II and the continued fear that they will be used again; the movement toward political independence on the part of scores of former colonies in Africa, Asia, and elsewhere; the revulsion felt over the brutalities of recent wars (especially the treatment of the Jews by Hitler's Germany); and the assassination of men of peace like Mahatma Gandhi, John F. Kennedy, Robert F. Kennedy, and Martin Luther King, Jr.

For reasons such as the above, plus many others, including the preaching of the Christian church and the revitalization of the great Asian religions (i.e., Vedanta; the Buddhist missions to Europe and America; etc.), the pitch or tone of ethical sensitivity has advanced to such a degree that it has made the leap or transition from accumulated quantity to that of a new quality —a unique ethical cast of mind that is positive, loving, and humanistic in the same way that the radical theology is.

The Central Axis of the New Morality

The central axis of this new ethical sensitivity is the communal or interpersonal relations aspect. It does not seem to be the outgoingness of a group of discrete or separate self-identical individual selves, but rather the mass sensitivity of a group made up of individual exemplars who are each at an equivalent ethical level. The communal aspect of the new morality is not unlike the blood-pressure rate or level in an interrelated group of organs that go to make up a physical organism. In short, there is a kind of extraordinary, extrasensory perception at work in this group ethical sensitivity. One does not need to be converted to the new outlook; one merely participates in it, one feels it. Anyone who has openmindedly visited a hippie community and talked with hippies will recognize the "feeling" I mention here.

There are some pertinent examples of this interparticipatory group sensitivity in the modern-day folk songs, such as "Blowin' in the Wind" and Ed Ames's "Who Will Answer?" These two songs express the absolute disgust and indignation of the younger generation—and of bearers of the new mentality of all ages—for the racial discrimination and the chronic warlikeness and escapism into drugs and alcohol of people of all classes in our society. These songs and the scores like them—such as "What Have They Done to the Rain?" (Joan Baez), "Waist Deep in the Big Muddy" (Pete Seeger), and "They Are Only a Pawn in Their Game" (Bob Dylan)—express the idealism and optimism of the new mentality, for such songs assume that all men are brothers, that they can live in peace and cooperation together—if only they will. We think immediately of the union songs of past decades that declared: "Because all men are brothers, the whole wide world around, one union shall unite us. . . ." The International Workers of the World are spiritual forebears of the new mentality. Selfishness, provincialism, particularity, partiality, nationality, racism (white and/or black) are all absent from such songs—except where they are attacked as demonizations and distortions of man's social, religious, and political heritage.

What we are trying to describe here is a kind of ethical noosphere, using that neologism in the sense that its author, Teilhard de Chardin, used it. Teilhard spoke of the development on the surface of the earth—through interpersonal and international contacts and rapid communications—of a growing single, unitary, intellectual consciousness, embracing all men across the face of the whole planet.[1]

All the signs discernible among the bearers of the new mentality, from buttons, songs, styles of life, books, articles, protests —and even riots on campuses—seem to indicate that this ethical noosphere (which we might term the "ethosphere") is a reality. It is exemplified in the world of experience and logical discourse. In plain speech, there are men and women today who feel alike and who think alike on a variety of related issues. Such men and women form the group I have designated by the phrase "bearers of the new mentality," and we might equally well designate them "bearers of the new morality." These people are not just separate individuals joined together by common interests and concerns. They are not examples of members of a "social contract," such as sect-group converts, or even card-carrying Communists or members of a political party or labor union. They have not joined together in any systematic way—unless the gathering of some of them in the East Village area of New York City or the Haight-Ashbury section of San Francisco can be called "organization." They have not made a temporary alliance with one another to affect the course of the government or the economy although some are active in the new left movement. The new mentality and its concomitant new morality embraces the political activists, to be sure, but it is far wider than the limited influence of S.D.S. and the college movement for Eugene McCarthy.

This new way of looking at the world is even far broader than the vast disaffection of citizens over the Vietnam war. Rather, the bearers of the new mentality are—each one—particular examples of a new species of human being that, as a group, shares one, unitary ethical (and/or moral) consciousness. To ignore the ethical message of this new consciousness in one place is simply to have to face it in another area. As the repressive measures taken by establishment groups during the civil rights struggle and by the police during the antiwar demonstrations so conclusively made manifest, to shoot down or imprison some member or members—exemplars of the new ethical sensitivity in one city or place—is merely to precipitate the rising of more exemplars in that very same place as well as to stimulate the conversion and creation of new exemplars elsewhere. The early Christians recognized this "creation by opposition" principle and used it to good effect. "The blood of the martyrs is the seed of the church" is a universal truth applicable not only to the church but to nations, ideas, and institutions of every type.

The new ethical sensibility we have called the new morality—the moral edge of the new mentality—can, by reason of what we have said above—never be defeated by the force of right, left, or center. This new sensibility must, at last, absorb all else into itself, and become the novel synthesis of all that was good in the older traditions of left and right. If we can but understand the decisive and keen moral fervor that animates this new moral vision, then we will be able to understand most of the problems (and see something of the solutions) related to human interpersonal and intrapersonal relationships. With Hegel and Marx we stand confident that history is on the side of the new mentality because the new mentality is nothing but the novel, progressive edge of mankind's spiritual history. The aims of this new mentality will be carried out, willingly or unwillingly, for these aims—brotherhood, personal and group self-fulfillment, universal love and peace—are the ultimate aims of man's spiritual progress. The new morality is, therefore, at once the voice of the historical group which bears it, as well as of the individual members of the group. In a manner analogous to the classical doctrine of God, the particularity of the new mentality and morality is its universality, and its universality is its particularity. The potentiality of the new form of consciousness is fully expressed in its actuality, while every finite, individual, and personal actuality now is transcended by its (future) potentiality.

The Content of the New Morality

Delbert L. Earisman, writing in *Hippies in Our Midst,* tells us something of the content of the new morality in his report of a talk with David, a young hippie in the East Village area of New York City.

David had been impressed by the spiritual poverty of middle-class culture, he said, when he was on his first full-time job, teaching in a school in a New York slum area. Visiting the home of one of his students, he noticed that a hungry little boy came to the door. The family invited the boy in and fed him, and he left. Nobody knew where he came from, where he was going, who he was. But they fed him. David had grown up in the suburbs in an area of sixty-thousand-dollar homes, and he remembered that when the neighborhood children were playing together at one of their houses and lunchtime came, the mother of the boy at whose house they were playing would send all the other boys home to their own mothers for lunch. "They weren't even strangers," he said. "They were my friends; we were there playing together, and yet in those sixty-thousand-dollar houses the people who had all the money just never thought of sharing a simple little thing like a lunch, and down in the slums anybody would share their food with you if you asked them." . . .

Like all other hippies, David practices free love; that is, he will stay with a girl for a while, perhaps a matter of months, then they will separate and find other partners. He assumes that sometime he will find a girl that he likes well enough to stay with permanently, and then he will marry her. But he also feels that his present style of life has removed all of the sexual tensions and anxieties that usually plague Western man. . . .

I saw David later that evening, strolling in the park with his girl friend—he called her his roommate—and they were casually talking and holding hands like any straight couple.[2]

Here was one inviting me to search his feelings any way I could, who deeply wished for me to understand him. The reason lay, perhaps, in the fact that I presented myself as simply and unashamedly straight—I was middle class and approaching middle age, and I had not smoked marijuana nor taken LSD. That is, in every respect but one I represented their parents' class and generation. The one respect in which I was different was that I was sitting on the grass in Tompkins Square Park, seriously listening to them. And they could tell me what they could not tell their own parents—that they took LSD, that they practiced free love, and that in spite of the way it might seem to the parents it was for the kids something religious and moral and the realest thing in the world.[3]

Earisman's fascinating and sympathetic study makes it clear that no matter what the older generation (with its "straight" mentality and hypocritical allegiance to "straight" morality) might think of the young, their drug experimentation and "free love" are—to them—preeminently religious and moral.

Earisman also reports that "the hippie ethic is simple. . . . 'Do your own thing, but don't try to put your thing onto anybody else.' "[4]

Indeed, as we have said earlier, the content of this ethical consciousness is simple and direct. It is the Golden Rule of all the higher religions: "Do unto others as you would have them do unto you." This positive, benevolent attitude toward life is akin to the concept of "reverence for life" taught by Albert Schweitzer, and it is both inner-directed ("unto you") and outer-directed ("do unto others") at one and the same time.

This new ethical sensitivity thus transcends the philosophical problem of the one and the many, the individual and society, as Jesus, Paul, the prophets, Confucius, and the Bhagavad-Gita's authors also transcended this philosophical riddle. For the bearers of the new mentality there is no separation in thought or act between the public and the private good. Paul's extended metaphor of the body[5] and its many different members in I Cor. 12:12–31 is a perfect description of a viewpoint that holds that all are brothers, and yet each should freely "do his own thing" (be prophets, be apostles, etc.).

However, the most amazing feature of the new mentality in ethics is its transcendence and progress beyond even the most sensitive of the older teachers—including Paul Tillich—because it has moved beyond the courage of doubt into the leap (or "risk") of affirmation. The new mentality's bearers are optimistic, and their ethical views are optimistic. One might call this new ethical concept a transcendental unity of the affirmation of one's own life and a reverence for the life of all other creatures. Thus the new morality is essentially a morality of life itself. It is religious, then, because it deals with the ultimate—with life—although its patterns of response can be described in purely empirical, naturalistic terms. This should cause us no problem, because churchmen have always confessed that God is in the world, and yet have considered the materialistic descriptions of the world by the physicist to be neutral—not atheistic.

The new morality, like the new mentality which forms its background and foundation, is an outgrowth of the normal evolutionary progress of Western man. This evolutionary progress has appeared to be "devolutionary" ("running down," not "building up") to many sensitive spirits for a long time, especially since the close of World War I. As a response of growing estrangement from the crumbling symbol foundations of Western culture, American society first produced the "fugitive" or expatriate generation (called the "lost" generation), then the beat generation, and now the hippie or "love" generation. Delbert L. Earisman has done such a sympathetic job of describing the twentieth-century movement "from lost generation to love generation" in his book[6] that I will not develop this part of the background of the new morality here. I prefer to approach the topic of the elements within American and Western European cultures which have provoked the rise of the new mentality through a discussion of a phenomenon that reflects elements of the lost, beat, and love generations—the camp movement.

Camp

The phenomenon that the press calls "camp" is actually a style of life that embraces many phenomena and that exists in both a purer and a more popular form. The essence of camp is the "put-on"; the tongue in cheek, sly poking of fun at our society and its supposed values. The sign of camp's presence is the subtle air of unreality; the baroque, overdone quality of its art and language. The camp "taste" is revealed in its apparent lack of taste. Camp is the deliberate and artful cultivation of an air of musty, 1890-ish, provincial dress, architecture, and manners. Or, camp is the parodying of the dress, "go to hell" attitude and mannerisms of the prohibition era. The movie *Bonnie and Clyde* is pure camp—right down to its macabre ending. Camp is a deliberate and difficult—not to mention costly—attempt to regress to the problems and responses of eras in the recent past. It is an unreal response to the current situation, in one way, but perhaps not in others. Camp, in its purer form, grows directly out of the "junkyard school" of sculpture, the unconsciousness-expressive school of painting of Jackson Pollock, the adoption of East Indian styles of dress and frontier beards and haircuts by the hippies, and the rejection of the status-seeking of middle-class suburbia. In its wider, more popular form, camp has influenced the dress and decoration, even something of the style of life, of the same middle-class suburbanites against whom it is directed. Perhaps this isn't surprising since there isn't much distance between collecting antiques and going camp.

If camp is the artful establishment of an air of illusion or unreality, through the use of objects, symbols, speech, and mannerisms of an era of the recent past, it is an honest attempt at the evocation of unreality, not just a fad. The fact is, for many of us in the generation that went to college in the 1950's (as well as the generation of the 1960's), nothing has ever seemed "real" since the beginning of World War II. Somehow the "unreality principle" has been at work in our "straight" (or mainline) culture so completely, for so long, that the evocation of unreality by the camp cultists is, paradoxically, a nostalgic return to a reality we have forever lost. Going camp in one's style of life—even going hippie—is analogous to going fundamentalistic in religion. Both movements are reactions against an intolerable present; both decisions are efforts at repristination, at returning again to something that had meaning in a simpler day, at a time when we were less mature and less scarred by life.

We could become too Hegelian here, but a closer examination of the cult of camp seems to reveal a motion toward a transcendent synthesis by "lifting up" the finer elements of the thesis and antithesis that have been locked in struggle. One thing is sure, for those who can even dimly recall the days before Pearl Harbor, nothing since then has seemed as "real" as those hard days of depression and national recovery. No matter how wealthy we may now be, no matter how "good" our larger money supply and improved technology has made our everyday lives, somehow life has seemed to lose its genuine quality. It is this apprehension—vague and unconsciously felt in many persons, consciously recognized and articulated by others—that has led to the feeling that the world is "going to hell," that "we ought to drop the bomb," or, conversely, that we ought to "tune in, turn on, and drop out." Between the older couple who join a Holiness church and the teen-agers who flock to the East Village there is a common bond—the sense that life today is senseless; that it is not real, but that by an act of conscious decision we can drop out of the race toward destruction and find reality again. Not just the lost reality of a misspent youth, or the idiotic waste of two or five years of war service, or the reality of human communication which has been more broken than aided by the mass media, but we can find the reality of the meaningfulness of the act of living itself. Our culture, from old

to young, from left to right, from white to black, mourns for a
lost good and will pay any price to recover it.

We might ask why the camp movement reacts only a very
little way on the time scale, moving back to the 1920's or 1890's
—or in some cases to the Revolutionary War period—rather
than going completely primitive. I think the answer is fairly
clear. In the analogy of the joining of a fundamentalist sect, we
have a hint. The fundamentalist or "old-time religion" sect is
not (despite some claims) a return in either polity, liturgy, or
doctrine to the early Christian church. In fact, most such sects
are not even close approximations to churches that existed at
the time of the Protestant Reformation. Rather, these sects do
often (not always) reflect a liturgy, polity, and doctrine that
was fairly typical in the period 1880–1890. The repristination
or return to purity of the fundamentalist is not a return to the
earliest days and forms of Christianity, therefore, but simply a
return to as close a period to our own which exhibited problems
and solutions to those problems which the anxiety-ridden, ideo-
logically oriented cultist can understand and accept.

For example, there is considerable brutality in our present
life-style. There are thousands of casualities in Vietnam, hundreds of injured and dead in our urban ghettos—all of which
disturbs the peace and even the life-style of every sensitive man
and woman. But in order to show the foolishness of violence,
without being considered subversive, we need to produce a
movie such as *Bonnie and Clyde*. By showing the foolishness
and pointlessness of violence in the recent past, we undermine
the appeal to violence today.

The Encyclopaedia Britannica 1968 *Book of the Year*[7]
featured a special report on "The Flower Children" which
quoted University of California sociologist Mark Messer's own
quote of a hippie:

We are not necessarily fashioning ourselves [the hippie said]
as a sort of anti-image to our parents. It's just that we have
grown up in an environment that was very, very different from
the Depression, and we're entirely different people.[8]

"Camp" was originally a slang term, just as "hippie" and "beat" are slang terms. In all three cases, these terms are derived from the alienated, more or less shadowy, elements of our culture. "Hip" and "hippie" grew out of the life-style and haunts of the jazz musicians, while "camp" very probably originated in the twilight world of homosexuality. The unreal quality of that "other side" of society makes it a fitting origin for the term and for the life-style it so well describes.

But why this sense of unreality? Why is the recent past (thirty-five years ago, for example) more "real"—or more understandable—than the experienced present? Apparently the reason is our sense of the inordinate "flying by" of time, at least from the standpoint of the growth and development of so many vital, dangerous, and complex things in such a short period of time. Time somehow seems foreshortened today. We are glutted, mentally and spiritually, with so much undigested progress made so quickly. We feel ourselves drowning in events—a condition that seems endemic in America—and even the normal rule. If it were only the psychic cripples who felt themselves in this undigested temporal way, there would be no problem. However, the sight of a president of the United States deciding not to run for office again because of his inability to handle and digest events shows us that the experience of the rush of time is a common phenomenon.

The recent past seems more real to us for another reason—an important one. The 1930's, for all their economic deprivation and crime waves, were times of international peace for America. Chicago and New York City may have heard the roar of submachine guns, as Saigon does now, but for the most part the gangsters fought among themselves. Perhaps the paycheck was cut, or even cut off, but Junior was not in combat on the Asian land mass. There is an air of unreality about war and wartime—even in a home country that has been fortunate enough to escape armed attack on the major portion of its national territory—and, in a real sense, America has been at war since the "armed neutrality" of 1940. Surely, those who can accept war and wartime

as real are the mentally disturbed ones. Those who reject war—
hot or cold—and its concomitant mental states as unreal must
be seen as the mentally healthy. The fact that more people are
not consciously aware of the illness of a "wartime" mentality
only reveals that not many of America's 200 million-plus citizens have actually experienced war at its worst—up close, over
a significant period of time. The bearers of the new mentality
have absorbed some of the abhorrence of war and warlikeness
that was gained in firsthand experience by many of their teachers
and the novelists, poets, and moviemakers who have genuinely
communicated with them.

There has been a state of warfare somewhere in the fabric
of human society since the beginning of recorded history. Every
high school and college student knows that the outline of history is largely an outline of the dates and results of "major"
battles. Some historians have observed that from the time of
Julius Caesar until now, only a few dozen years have been
years of "universal" peace within the Western family of nations.
The twentieth century, then, has been like every other century
before it—with the exception that our century has progressed to
a point where almost every nation of the world is led or pushed
into participation in "world wars." Although there were some
neutrals in both World War I and World War II, those conflicts
did carry battle and destruction to every quarter of the globe.
Since 1945, with the victories over Germany and Japan, there
has been no true peace. One estimate is that there have been
forty-eight "small" or "limited" wars since VJ day. When we
bracket World War II with the Spanish Civil War (1936, before)
and the Berlin Crisis (1948, after), then go on to Korea (1950–
1953), Malaya, Israel (three wars), Hungary, Suez, East Germany, the off-shore islands (Formosa), Algeria, Indochina
(1946–1954), the Congo, Cuba, Dominican Republic, and now
Vietnam, we see that ours is a time of very "warm" war.

The new mentality has come to consciousness in those who
bear it during this period of anxiety, hostility, and fear of death.
Those who think in the new way react, in their "new morality,"

out of a sense of sickness over war. The sensitive are frankly amazed that so much of straight or main-line society has become "used" to war. To the bearer of the new mentality, America today seems very much like *1984,* where war has become peace and peace is called war. This insight is not limited to the left in America, but is a reaction shared by the right as well; only in the case of the right, there is a neurotic reaction that desires to gain "peace" by dropping "the bomb" on "them." Such an attitude—"peace through war"—would be a topic for psychologists only if it were not the public position of some United States politicians. The strategy of "peace through war" seems to be the ideology of these leaders as well as of a large part of the American public, all of whom have forgotten that "he who lives by the sword shall die by the sword." The bearers of the new mentality recognize the truth of that proverb.

Violence in America

Contemporary sociologists and psychologists are reminding us of something we should all recognize from our history courses and from our television viewing: America is a violent country. World War II, after all, was preceded in the United States by the era of gang warfare, the protection racket, prohibition raids, and bank robberies. Ours is perhaps the best armed society in the history of the world. Estimates put the number of private arms in the United States at over 100 million, at least one gun for every two citizens. In some neurotic way, the average citizen sees himself as still living on the Western frontier, where all went armed and the civil law was weak. The current "gun craze" only underscores this fantasy.

The gun craze to which we refer includes the rejection by the National Rifle Association of the major elements included in proposed state and federal legislation against commerce in guns. For example, the so-called "Kennedy bill" (after Senator Ted Kennedy) was designed to restrict the sale of hand guns and also the sale by mail of rifles, such as the cheap rifle used to kill

President John F. Kennedy. However, the N.R.A. lobby effectively watered down many of the restrictions proposed in this law, which, in modified form, then was passed into law in 1968.

The N.R.A. usually bases its case for free and easy gun laws, particularly on rifles and shotguns, on the Bill of Rights which guarantees the right of the people "to keep and bear arms." In 1968, a poster appeared in hardware-store windows all over the country proclaiming "Protect Your Right to Keep and Bear Arms." Unfortunately, the N.R.A. and its friends often fail to note that this proviso is included so that there will be "a well-regulated militia." In point of fact, this right means that the states have the right (and duty) to maintain an emergency defense force, what we have come to call a National Guard. Surely such an institution is valuable and needed, but just as surely, a well-regulated militia does not need to order used, imported rifles by mail from private arms houses. In reality, if the sale by mail of rifles were prohibited, there would be less need for the services of the National Guard.

The current gun craze has arisen as a neurotic response to the increase in violence in the American Negro's drive for a genuine enjoyment of his civil rights. Both sides of this controversy, the Negro radicals and the white reactionaries, have indulged in massive armaments movements. In a tragic example of opposite and equal errors at work, the black radicals have armed for "insurrection" and the Ku-Klux Klan, as well as lower and lower-middle-class reactionary whites in general, has armed for "defense." The present-day American situation is much like that between the Greek Cypriot and Turkish Cypriot communities, or like the armaments race between the Allies and the Central Powers in pre-1914 Europe. One does not have to be a pessimist to state that few swords have been beaten into plowshares before they were beaten over men's heads. Preparing to fight and fighting are but different stages of the same process. Right now, with the Minute Men, the Ku-Klux Klan, the Deacons for Defense, and the Black Nationalists all moving about storing and learning to use arms, there are probably more private armies in America than there were in Germany after World War I. Chaos is chaos whether it comes from right or left, white or black, and the bearers of the new mentality call on all to examine the chaotic core of the American spirit.

The Guerrilla and the Sniper

In some psychotic few the gun craze builds up into gun madness. Perhaps the distinctive individual type to emerge in the twentieth century is the guerrilla fighter. He has been made into a hero by the existentialists of France (Sartre and Camus were resistance fighters), and glorified by writers like Ernest Hemingway in dramas, movies, novels, and short stories. Unfortunately, the Western world discovered, after 1945, that guerrillas fight for all sorts of causes—as France found in Algeria and Indochina. Today, the guerrilla has hit a nadir with the American establishment and middle class because of the tenacity and fighting qualities of the Viet Cong overseas and because of the chilling danger to the public and police of the sniper in the urban ghettos. The sniper and the Viet Cong, taken together, are apt symbols of the deep problems in which America is embroiled today.

But the sniper—as a symbol of cultural breakdown and meaninglessness—goes deeper even than the seemingly bottomless war in Southeast Asia and the complex problems of race relations at home. The sniper has emerged as a distinct psychotic type: the mindless, random, motivationless mass murderer, who kills large numbers of people in a tragic act of societal rejection. Although there have been some assassinations of American president in the past (we do have a violent history—the Civil War was no debate), the murder of John F. Kennedy seems to have pulled the psychological cork that has unleashed a terrible flow of sickness and hate all over America. Jack Ruby's televised murder of Lee Harvey Oswald ripped open the psychic wound in the American spirit even wider. That wound apparently is still draining the positive energy and happiness from much of American life.

Perhaps, in a perverted, black-mass way, the American culture, aware of its meaninglessness, is drifting toward violence as a (sick) way to achieve self-purgation. Perhaps the "blood theology" of the great nineteenth-century revivals lingers still in the American consciousness, and each of us moves actively or passively toward redemption through suffering and death. The Negro in the inner city who rebels against the invisible walls which cut him off from full participation in the national life we can understand, if not excuse. The Negro rioter reacts savagely out of a sense of frustration and moral outrage. The violence of the reactionary whites who kill Negroes and civil rights workers is less understandable, and yet the fact of racial hatred and the supposed threat to white identity is well established. But the mindless, warningless murder of a multitude such as the shootings from the Texas tower and the slaying of the nurses in Chicago we cannot understand at all. In a similar way, we find the murder of the preacher of peace, Martin Luther King, Jr., equally senseless, even if it were done by racial bigots. Perhaps the only generality we can draw from all of this is that America—except for the bearers of the new mentality—is drifting toward a style of life characterized by Balkan-type violence.

The Increasing Role of Drugs in the Life-Style

The bearers of the new mentality, who are developing the outlines of a new morality, are quite aware of the problems and dangers of drug use. As much as a sympathetic observer might want to depreciate it, drugs are the one distinctive element of the hippie subculture. By drugs we mean chiefly marijuana ("pot" or "grass") and LSD, although there is also a long history and a growing use of various pep pills and other drugs, such as STP and "speed."[9] There does not seem to be very much of a problem with the "hard" or "body" drugs, such as heroin. The hippie generation is not the first such grouping to be formed around attraction to (including interest in, not necessarily the use of) drugs. The beat generation of the late 1940's and early 1950's was also interested in marijuana. But the beat generation was also a group hooked on alcohol and it experimented with the "hard" drugs. So, too, was the "lost" or expatriate generation. The hard-drinking Ernest Hemingway symbolizes that post-World War I group. The hippie generation, however, is not that hooked on alcohol. Outside of beer-drinking and the occasional bottle of wine, the true hippie has no need for alcohol. In one way, marijuana, although now illegal, is not as dangerous as liquor. Marijuana does not build up a tolerance for its effects so that more and more of it is needed for a "high" each time it is used. And finally, marijuana does not cause a hangover. Pot smokers describe the day after a marijuana party as one in which everything is experienced as "mellow yellow."

In point of fact, there is increasing literature by both medical and legal experts who hold that marijuana should be legalized. These advocates of reform insist that the laws against marijuana are not needed, since it does not become addictive and has no more serious effects upon the user than does alcohol. Moreover, the present laws cause persons who would experiment with drugs to fall under the influence of gangsters who make tremendous profits selling marijuana. Much more importantly, the harassment of the pot smoker only frustrates the efforts needed to control the dangerous drugs such as heroin, and perhaps LSD, STP, and speed.

Unfortunately, there is a vast credibility gap in the efforts of some law enforcement agencies to combat the use of drugs. For example, a medical doctor holding a state staff position in Pennsylvania misled the public sometime ago by claiming that six college students had blinded themselves by staring at the sun while under the influence of LSD. This announcement caused such a public reaction that the attorney general and the governor of the state instituted an investigation. It was discovered that none of this had taken place. To the credit of the governor, he exposed the fraud. One wonders just how many "lies in the interest of the truth" have been and are being told about the use of drugs.

The Middle-Class Pill Culture

Drug use is hardly confined to the hippie subculture. Drugs are an increasing problem for all segments of contemporary American society, but perhaps especially for the college-age group and the middle class. The hippie button that proclaims "LSD—Better Living Through Chemistry" is a pun that cuts across both the straight society and the dropout subculture. The movie *Valley of the Dolls* showed with a crushing intensity the overuse of chemistry's gifts of better living. One need not be a medical doctor or druggist to know that our country has a middle-class pill culture. The very executives who cluck and criticize the hippies for smoking marijuana do so while puffing cigarettes (nicotine), drinking bourbon and water (alcohol), and taking tranquilizers. Among the college-age youth, the use of pep pills to keep themselves awake while studying or "at their best" over long weekend parties, joined with a dependence on weight-reducing pills in the case of girls, probably constitutes a more serious health problem than the use of liquor or marijuana. Conversations with many high school and college students reveal the fact that such pills are readily available to young people at many drugstores without prescription or can be gotten through easy "contacts."

The effects of LSD on human beings over a long period of time are still relatively unknown, since the drug was discovered only in 1943. What is known includes the facts that the use of LSD can precipitate psychosis in some highly repressed subjects (and we are all repressed to some degree), and may cause chromosome damage. Such damage would result in defective children—a horrible situation to contemplate. Under these circumstances, all responsible people should work to bring about effective and reasonable educational efforts to make known these dangers and to institute reasonable controls on LSD. However, the middle class, with its drinking, smoking, and tranquilizing, should remember that only he who is without sin should cast the first stone. One wonders if drugs would be so tempting if our young people had not been reared in such drug-oriented households.

Protesting and Dropping Out

One of the major activities of masses of people all over the world since the end of World War II has been protesting. Picketing, rallying, voting, shouting, letter-writing—all these actions have been raised to the status of fine arts by Asians, Africans, South and Central Americans, American Negroes, and university students throughout America and the world. Many times protests have degenerated—or devolved—into armed or unarmed combats between the protestors and the police, militia and/or army. Ours is a time when political sophistication is growing among the masses. Men are becoming aware that they can better their positions in life if they struggle to do so. But there is another side of this sophistication—the passive protest of dropping out. By retiring to their own selected "Walden Ponds," men and women are turning their backs upon a society they consider "gone mad." Dropping out we must fully understand is a positive—although passive—protest against things as they are. It is a kind of spiritual and intellectual nonviolent resistance.

Positive Negativity

In a multitude of ways Lao-tzu, the ancient Chinese philosopher, was right when he wrote, "The Tao that can be spoken is not the eternal Tao."

What did he mean? He meant that the truth can never be brought to full expression; the real can never fully be grasped; the beautiful can never be completely possessed. The ancient

Hebrew teacher Jesus, called the Christ, also expressed this thought in his justly famous words, "He who would save his life will lose it; and he that loses his life (for the sake of the truth) will possess it eternally."

Albert Camus, a contemporary French existentialist writer, saw this same configuration in reality and spoke of life as being absurd, but precious and worthwhile, not in spite of, but just because of, life's ultimate absurdity. Jean-Paul Sartre, a tougher-minded existentialist, has expressed this insight by declaring that man has no essence, he is precisely nothing, and out of this nothingness man—as a self-elected project—is to create himself.

What has all this to say to our theme, "Dropping Out" and "Positive Negativity"? Much, as we shall see, for men protest whenever their human sensitivities and sensibilities are ridden over roughshod by those who try to absolutize the tao, i.e., life, the true, the beautiful, the good, and the just, into dehumanizing systems. Men protest precisely when the human, the unaccountable, the absurd, the "holy" elements in life are overlooked and even suppressed. This is why such protest is a positive negativity, for it seeks to build these human values again and not destroy anything essential to man.

Such was the existential occasion that brought Søren Kierkegaard into the lifelong battle he fought against the rationalistic, middle-class acceptance of Hegel's philosophical system—which was believed by many intellectuals in the nineteenth century to equate true Christianity with good (European) citizenship. It was a protest against the loss of the individual in the mass movements of a historical process, which even Hegel recognized was a "slaughter bench" on which the individual was destroyed by the vast, deep workings of the Spirit who was coming to consciousness in the movements of history.

It is this dehumanization and loss of the individual that has prompted Gabriel Marcel, the Catholic Christian existentialist, to speak of the twentieth century as a "broken world" in which men have become silent adjuncts to their efficient (and non-human) machines.

It is this process which forced Albert Camus—who saw the effects of our age's brutalization of man's human feelings in the brutality of the Algerian War—to urge modern men to revolt in his books *The Plague, The Rebel, The Stranger,* and *Resistance, Rebellion, and Death.* This same situation of the loss of human sensitivity was the occasion behind Jesus' denunciation of the Pharisees of his day. "You have perverted the word of God for the sake of your tradition."

It was just such a feeling of revulsion from dehumanization, from the feelings of our own inadequacy, that prompted Socrates —the man who claimed to know nothing—to drink the hemlock rather than to "cease being a philosopher" even though he might have to suffer many deaths.

And it was in protest against such demonization of the holy, against such dehumanization of religion and ethics, that forced Jesus to revolt—and to cleanse the Temple with a whip—and led directly to his death on the cross.

The Forms of Feeling Are Dead

In a genuine way, the declaration that God is dead, that the institutions of our society are dead or dying (the church, nationalism, etc.), and that our traditional morality is dead, really means that the forms of feeling which these symbols and symbol-bearing institutions once "contained" have dried up. The emotional and spiritual content is dead, and hence, the symbols are destroyed—not "broken" and understood, but smashed and dead.

Hundreds of thousands, even scores of millions of American, Canadian, and Western European citizens still "think" they "believe in" the traditional symbols of Christianity, but the number of people who feel, deep down, that they do so believe must be much smaller. I think it is important to recognize that the appropriate response to a religious symbol and to a religious doctrine—which is the verbalization of the inner meaning of the symbol—is a feeling of trust, acceptance, and open response.

No matter how hard the literalists (who are holdovers from eighteenth-century rationalism) may talk about rational and intellectual acceptance of the Scriptures and doctrines, the religious response is not primarily an intellectual one. Schleiermacher's great genius lies in his recognition of the psychoemotional basis of the religious experience. The religious personality comes in every possible variety, from John Wesley's simple and crude coal miners to the intellectuals of the Oxford movement and T. S. Eliot, but the essence of their religiousness lies on another plane than the conscious—or even the mental—one.

However, millions living today still know the words—and recognize the sacred symbols—while being more or less consciously (but certainly, unconsciously) aware that the feelings, the music, behind the words and symbols have departed. "Ichabod" might be a good name for this inner-alienated Western "Christian"; for him "the glory has departed" (I Sam. 4:21).

This inner lack of feeling has brought about many attempts by partly secularized Christians to recapture the feelings of transcendence, benevolence, community, and peace that have evaporated. Some of these attempts include: the liturgical revival in various Protestant churches (especially the Lutheran and the Episcopal churches); the liturgical experimentation among very liberal Roman Catholics and in the "underground churches"; the introduction of "folk masses" and other "modern" media into worship; and the large number of "modern speech" translations of the New Testament.

Perhaps the greatest efforts to recover the "forms of feeling" have been in the areas of preaching and social activism—not the preaching taught by the professors of homiletics at seminaries, to be sure, but the individual attempts of thousands of sensitive ministers, priests, and rabbis in America and Europe who have responded positively to the problems of meaninglessness and the violence that follows it with sermons directed squarely at the emptiness within the lives of the people around them. The preaching of Paul Tillich, as recorded in *The Shaking of the Foundations, The New Being,* and other volumes,[10] represents just such an attempt. The preaching, too, of Helmut Thielicke[11] in Germany has this same inner, existential aim. The lectures of Bishop James A. Pike, the "talks" of Malcolm Boyd, and the works of Bishop J. A. T. Robinson also reflect an attempt to say something helpful to the drifting masses of men in the twentieth century. Compared with the number of those who speak cogently on matters of war, race relations, and changing sexual mores, there are literally hundreds of thousands of Western clergymen who do not speak to their people but who repeat the worn-out formulas of the past. Among these representatives of the past must, in honesty, be included the great names in evangelism, such as Billy Graham.

In the arena of social action we find the genuine cutting edge of the attempt to recover the forms of feeling in religious symbolism again. As we have discussed this involvement in the civil rights and peace movements before, we shall omit further comment here.

The Form and Suggested Content of a Truly New Morality

Fundamentally man is the desire to be, and the existence of this desire is not to be established by an empirical induction; it is the result of an *a priori* description of the being of the for-itself (man). . . . There is not first a single desire of being, then a thousand particular feelings, but the desire to be exists and manifests itself only in and through jealousy, greed, love of art, cowardice, courage, and a thousand contingent, empirical expressions which always cause human reality to appear to us only as manifested by a particular man, by a specific person.[12]

But ontology and existential psychoanalysis . . . must reveal to the moral agent that he is the being by whom values exist. It is then that his freedom will become conscious of itself and will reveal itself in anguish as the unique source of value and the nothingness by which the world exists.[13]

The form of the new morality is idealistic, in the finest,

popular sense of that term. It is overflowing with optimism about
the basic qualities of man, who is seen to be naturally inclined
to "do his own thing" and to allow others to do likewise. The
form of the new morality is thus a permissive, nonrepressive
exhortation to men and women to live by a standard of positive
love: living as we would freely live, and assisting others to so
live freely also. This basic love attitude is to develop into care
and concern for one another. We find it necessary to speak of
the form of the new morality rather than of its content, because
essentially the new morality has no specific, universalized (or
generalized) content beyond the impulse, and exhortation, to
love one another. Beyond this positive, active benevolence of
spirit, there remains only an empirical appraisal of the manifold
situations into which all men are continuously moving. The circumstances of each varied and unique situation are weighed
and a judgment is then made as to "what love would do" in this
situation.

I have tried to express the insights of the new morality in a
few lines of free verse. The new morality—as an expression of
a new form of Christianity—

> Refuses to gloss over the neurotic
>   irrationality of people;
> Refuses to excuse laziness, meanness,
>   spite, and prejudice on the basis of ignorance;
> Rejects pride, but demands self-respect;
> Rejects moralism, but requires purity—
> (Purity—the doing of the natural;
> Moralism—the repression of actions
>   men, being born, must do).
> The new morality
>   sees in tension, anxiety, dislike, meaninglessness,
>   and unhappiness
> The very sin Jesus died (and lives in us) to overcome.[14]

Specifically, the new morality holds that, while men's offenses
against one another are certain to come (men sin and act "im-

morally" every day), the moralist should attempt to overcome the evil effects of the offense, and thus salvage the most good for all concerned (including the offender) out of the situation. Damning and condemning the offender may actually aggravate the evil effects of the situation—in some cases, perhaps many—while in other situations it may serve an educational function and thus lead to good.

The exact nature of the "solution" to a moral "problem," handled by way of the insights of the new morality, is always vague and tentative at the beginning. The tentativeness serves to sharply define the new approach from—at least the popular conception of—the older morality. The new moralist doesn't begin by defining just what rules have been broken and calling for immediate repentance and/or punishment—at least not every time.

Martin E. Marty, distinguished church historian at the Divinity School of the University of Chicago and associate editor of *The Christian Century,* observed in the June, 1967, *Playboy* panel discussion on "Religion and the New Morality":

We are being forced to look at every aspect of environment in new ways, and a radical reappraisal of human relationships is inevitable. So far, no newly clarified formulation of morality has come during this change. We don't know enough about how the Christian message relates to these "new people" to give them clear guidance. This doesn't shock or surprise or shatter me. The Christian Church has often had to bide time or tread water. Take the example of modern contraception. Here, as in so many other instances, there is no detailed, ready-to-go Christian ethic tucked away in our files, waiting to be put to use.[15]

In the same panel discussion, Harvey Cox, of Harvard Divinity School, discussed the "newness" of the new morality, stressing that the current reappraisal in morality is precisely what a living morality must continuously be undergoing. Cox remarked:

Morality is always new, always changing, because there are always new situations emerging to which existing moral principles have to be applied, and this requires new thinking. The trouble is, as Bishop Robinson pointed out, that for some people, new morality means no morality. Morality is a living changing organism; it has to be.[16]

The one firm principle of the new morality, as we have observed above, which is the major portion of the form of the new approach and its chief content, was expressed by Bishop J. A. T. Robinson in *Honest to God,* in these words:

For nothing can of itself always be labelled as 'wrong'. One cannot, for instance, start from the position 'sex relations before marriage' or 'divorce' are wrong or sinful in themselves. . . . *The only intrinsic evil is lack of love.*[17]

In actuality, how can any Christian, Jew, Muslim, Hindu, Buddhist, the religionist of any faith, or humanist object to the basing of moral judgment upon love? The Golden Rule, as we mentioned earlier, is found in all the great religions, and it forms part of the ethics of every recognized philosophy. The *Playboy* interviewer mentioned one very real reason why the new morality has been so severely condemned by traditionalist churchmen:

The sexual revolution represents more of a change in attitudes than in actions. Many liberal churchmen feel that it is precisely this change in moral values, rather than any change in overt sexual practices, that threatens traditional churchmen, because it signifies their loss of power over the minds and emotions of men.[18]

This loss of power has been mounting with every decade since about 1850, despite small reverses of losses during the revivalistic period of the last quarter of the nineteenth century and during the "return to religion" in the United States after World War II. This loss of power has gone so far now that the kind of power such clergymen want to exercise is efficacious only among the very young and the very ignorant. Actually, the loss of this power represents a victory for Christian liberty—no matter how traditionalists may define it.

Dr. Allen J. Moore, dean of students at the Claremont, California, School of Theology, observed during the same *Playboy* panel discussion:

Actually . . . the moral revolution is primarily a revolution of attitudes rather than actions. I'm not convinced that there is a great increase in sexual immorality today, even by Christian standards. We shouldn't mistake more openness, more freedom of discussion, greater tolerance, for a change in practice.[19]

The change in attitudes mentioned here has certainly taken place in the lives of many today. This change, from a concern for principles and institutions to a concern for persons and one's relationships to persons, forms one of the major elements of the new mentality.

The Search
for New Meaning

*T*HE experience of meaninglessness that has as its chief
symbol the declaration that God is dead has been dawning
upon Western mankind for over a century. The ever-increasing
numbers of people who lost all faith in the traditional philosophical doctrine of personal immortality—taught by idealism
and used by the Christian church—and who became increasingly
skeptical over the dogma of resurrection added to this sense of
the pointlessness of human life. Western man experienced a
debilitation of psychic energy as he passed through various crises
of faith. Matthew Arnold (1822–1888), the English poet, expressed this sense of loss in these words:

> The Sea of Faith
> Was once, too, at the full, and round earth's shore
> Lay like the folds of a bright girdle furl'd.
> But now I only hear
> Its melancholy, long, withdrawing roar,
> Retreating, to the breath
> Of the night-wind, down the vast edges drear
> And naked shingles of the world.[1]

Alfred, Lord Tennyson (1809–1892), also recognized the
age's growing loss of faith, but strove to replace the lost elements
with a liberal Christian humanism. In his poem "Oh Yet We
Trust" he dared to hope that the inner meaning of the old religious symbols could still be true:

> Oh yet we trust that somehow good
> Will be the final goal of ill.
>
> . . . .
>
> That nothing walks with aimless feet;
> That not one life shall be destroyed,
> Or cast as rubbish to the void,
> When God hath made the pile complete.[2]

In "Ring Out, Wild Bells," Tennyson affirmed the liberal faith that the new century, the twentieth century, would prove to be "the Christian century":

> Ring out false pride in place and blood,
> The civic slander and the spite;
> Ring in the love of truth and right,
> Ring in the common love of good.
>
> Ring out old shapes of foul disease,
> Ring out the narrowing lust of gold;
> Ring out the thousand wars of old,
> Ring in the thousand years of peace.
> Ring in the valiant man and free,
> The larger heart, the kindlier hand;
> Ring out the darkness of the land,
> Ring in the Christ that is to be.[3]

If we were not so fully committed to the same optimistic faith, it would be easy to parody Tennyson. The true extent of the growth of meaninglessness, the power of negation and destruction, in Western culture can be seen by examining each of Tennyson's hopes and then observing what became of those hopes in seven decades of twentieth-century history.

First, "the false pride in place and blood," by which Tennyson meant the dying aristocracy and the growing nationalism of his day, has grown into a Hydra-headed monster in the twentieth century. Nationalism and racism have plunged the world into war after war and now threaten to destroy many of the Western nations from within as well as from without. The "false pride in blood" of Nazism brought on the most extensive war—so far

—in human history, and a similar false pride in blood has brought America to the brink of racial war. "The civic slander and the spite" that Tennyson denounces might well be taken as a title for the political attacks on public officials in America and Europe in the twentieth century. Similar slander and spite have been shown by officials to their opponents.

Tennyson's prayer that "old shapes of foul disease" might disappear in the new century gives us the one bright spot in our analysis. Many of the old diseases have been conquered or contained since 1900. Unfortunately, the wars and exploitation of peoples of our era have caused even the worst of the old diseases to sometime reappear. The dreaded bubonic plague has arisen in Vietnam's protracted conflict, for example. The most serious deficiency in the modern period's war on disease, however, has been our failure to wipe out the disease of self-perpetuating poverty. That foul disease is as bad today as it was in Tennyson's day. All the vast schemes to raise the conditions of the poor to higher levels seem to be like sieves, picking up a few and letting the majority trickle back to their former places. The economic miracles of the West have enlarged the "have classes," but rather than destroying poverty have simply hidden it, until it speaks out in rage.

"The narrowing lust of gold" is still with us. Despite the victories of the British Labour Party, the coming of the New Deal and the Fair Deal (and the "Great Society") to the United States, there has been no relief from the lust for profit which drives the basic economy of the West on and on to new production (and profit) records, and on and on to chronically reoccurring problems. One wonders if this demonization of economic resources will be overcome as long as the maximization of profits remains an article of economic faith.

However, it is in reference to "the thousand wars of old," which Tennyson, like most Victorians, felt were forever behind mankind, that Tennyson's optimistic vision has proved most defective. "The thousand years of peace" have not dawned, and, to be realistic, seem more remote now than they did in the

1880's. Two world wars and hundreds of smaller ones have shown us the foolishness of the liberal belief that the twentieth century could become "the Christian century."

From Tennyson's liberal optimism and Arnold's liberal regret over the passing of "the Sea of Faith," it was possible to pass to the pessimism and sensuality of A. C. Swinburne (1837–1909). Swinburne, looking at his age, declared:

> From too much love of living,
> From hope and fear set free,
> We thank with brief thanksgiving
> Whatever gods may be
> That no life lives forever;
> That dead men rise up never;
> That even the weariest river
> Winds somewhere safe to sea.[4]

It is with the "war poets" that the full burden of the tragic meaninglessness brought on by the breakdown of Western civilization becomes profoundly manifest. Wilfred Owen (1893–1918) declared:

> If you could hear, at every jolt, the blood
> Come gargling from the froth-corrupted lungs,
> Bitter as the cud
> Of vile, incurable sores on innocent tongues,—
> My friend, you would not tell with such high zest
> To children ardent for some desperate glory,
> The old lie: *Dulce et decorum est*
> *Pro patria mori.*[5]

The meaningfulness of life was largely drained away by the million-multiplied experiences of the Wilfred Owens of every nation in 1914–1918 and 1939–1945. In every other year of our century, from the hills of Korea to the Bay of Pigs to Dien Bien Phu to Da Nang, other men—and those who loved them—have come to the same insight. The blood of meaning has been drained from the body of our culture—drained off through the millions upon millions of physical wounds and psychic traumas brought on by the madness of men in a century of total war.

The Meaninglessness of Meaninglessness

It has been a long time since the days of which Wilfred Owen wrote: World War I and its aftermath. Indeed, today's younger generation must look back on that time (fifty years ago) in a manner not unlike the way we all look back—through history—at the American Civil War. Actually, the current college generation—and those under thirty in general—does not know anything firsthand about World War II. For those under thirty even Korea was an experience that took place far away when they were age twelve or younger. In short, the kind of meaninglessness, which we will here equate with a severe loss of values, that grew out of the experiences of wars in the recent past is simply not part of the new mentality of the younger generation.

Our War

Our present younger generation does have its war, however, a war that has been going on in some newsworthy degree since 1961. But this war, Vietnam, is not an occasion for the feeling of meaninglessness in the existentialist sense we have discussed above. Rather, Vietnam has revealed the deadness and emptiness of many traditional Western symbols and has set the bearers of the new mentality to the task of discovering what, for them, are the real meanings in life. The student protests against the war, against the draft, against the neglect of domestic social needs because of armed adventures abroad, all show a commitment to new meanings in life—although those new meanings may actually be redefined and rededicated old values such as universal love, brotherhood, and peace.

The search for the "real" or "inner" or even "new" meanings of the old symbols is a present-day fact. The younger generation, or at least that part of it which bears the new mentality, is searching for the roots of a set of values that will enable men to realize their own inner possibilities fully while living together in peace. The new search for genuine "forms of feeling" (i.e.,

genuine meaning) by the young today is seen in their adoption
of so many features of the Hindu philosophy of Vedanta (seen
especially in the interest in the Maharishi Mahesh Yogi a few
years ago); by their interest (for many years now) in Zen
Buddhism; and by the religious connotations given to the experience of taking various drugs.[6]

A basic reason for the search for meaning by the young today
is their recognition of the affectation of so much "literary existentialism." The whole experience of meaninglessness and existential anxiety[7] has been overdone by too many parlor existentialists in lectures, articles, and books. "Parlor" or "literary"
existentialism is the faddish approach to Sartre, Camus, and
Kierkegaard characteristic of many churchmen and academic
people. The whole business of crying that all meaning has gone
from modern life has become somewhat "cute" in the sense that
a child is "cute" when he repeats words and behavior over and
over that have previously brought him parental adulation. Perhaps the younger generation is really more adult than its elders.

Three Ways of Responding to the World

Our general knowledge of psychological processes and forces
would lead us to expect that the current search for new (or
renewed) meanings of the traditional symbols of Western culture would be colored in each case by the basic direction or
proclivities of the personalities involved. Under this insight, we
would see that those oriented to the past will search for the real
or inner meaning of symbols and confessions, while those oriented to the present might wish merely to clarify what the symbols can and do mean now. Persons oriented to the future might
be expected to show more radicality, searching for some new
meanings, or even new symbols, to guide man in the further
building up of our common culture.

Perhaps we can illustrate the personality coloration given to
the search for meaning by an analogy from biology. Life has
been defined, by biologists, as the presence of irritability; of

response to stimuli on the part of an organism. Life is certainly more than response to stimuli, but it is at least that, even in the highly complex—and transcendent—dimension of human being-ness (referred to in German existentialism as *Dasein*). Human beings respond to their environment through many dimensions, from the cellular to the organic to the unconscious to the intel-lectual and spiritual dimensions. An almost infinite number of different responses to the varied stimuli are possible and have become actual through the billions of lives that make up the history of the human race. Nothing is more paradoxical, nothing shows more novelty and creativity, than the responses of human beings to the stimuli of problems and challenges they meet in life. And yet, human responses tend to fall into general patterns which may be conveniently named "open" and "closed" re-sponses. For example, if someone thrust something toward you with the obvious intention of your taking it in your hand, an opening of your hand to receive the something would be an "open" response; while moving your hand away (perhaps in fear that you were being handed a hot coal!) would be a "closed" response. An insight gained from this example is that one must (and does) respond to stimuli of necessity—even ig-noring a stimuli amounts to a closed response, or a rejection. Stimuli affect us if we are living; only the dead do not respond.

The two basic patterns of response have almost infinite vari-eties of actual responses, to be sure. However, they reveal a structural similarity in that the first pattern is a positive, affirma-tive, trusting kind of response; while the second pattern is a negative, rejecting, untrusting kind of response. Obviously, the manifold problems and stimuli of life demand both kinds of responses, and the organism that continues to live makes more or less appropriate kinds of responses. Human beings, freed by technological developments from survival-level problems in many areas of their lives, often fall into a fairly fixed pattern of responses. People, then, often respond as open or closed per-sonalities to problems in the human dimension (history) whether such responses are appropriate or not. There arise in history, therefore, two basic personality types: the conservative (or closed) type and the radical (or open) type. The liberal type of response, and by extension the liberal type of personality and group, represents an intellectually determined, balanced admixture of open and closed responses. Human history, then, reveals these three major optional patterns of human response: the positive, the negative, and the synthesis of the two in human freedom.

Two Ways of Grasping the World

The present postexistentialistic age has its typical pattern of positive and negative human responses. What Heraclitus, the ancient wise man whose philosophy was big enough to embrace all opposites as manifestations of a basic unity, called two ways of grasping after wisdom have become polarized in our day.

On the positive, open, radical side of the polarity we have the veterans of the beat generation (Jack Kerouac, Norman Mailer, Allen Ginsberg, and a host of middle-aging others); the hippies, the teeny-boppers, and the yippies[8]; the new left students of S.D.S. and the remainders of the civil rights movement; the peace demonstrators and the conscientious objectors; the followers of Indian gurus and Alan Watts-type Zen Buddhists; and, finally, the "death of God" theologians and their campus chaplain, religion professor, and student followers.

On the negative, closed, conservative side of the fundamental polarity there are the security seekers of all ages, races, classes, and conditions who basically care for nothing but themselves, symbolized for them in the desire for money, what money can buy, and for the guaranteeing of its continued inflow.

A century like the twentieth which has experienced extreme changes in all aspects of human life would be expected to show, in the life-style of its people, extremes of human responses to those changes. The twentieth century does not disappoint either the historian or the sociologist, since it exhibits a degree of radically extreme responses that rival the best and worst responses of the era of the French Revolution and the period of the Renaissance. In politics alone, the twentieth century has exhibited a radical shift from the autocratic monarchy of the czars in Russia to the anarchy of the Russian civil war to the tyranny of the Communist Party over the same land of Russia. In America the political scene shifted from the reactionary conservatism and imperialistic expansion of the early decades (1898–1912) to the turmoil and socialization of the depression era and the New Deal to the era of the good feeling of the Eisenhower years to the civil strife of the late 1960's.

In morality in the United States the extreme "closeness" of the lingering Victorian era of the early decades of the twentieth century has shifted to the good times and moral laxness of the jazz era, through the social madness of the prohibition era (perhaps because of the efforts of the religious and social conservatives to suppress vice), to the breakdown of much more of the traditional morality during and after World War II. Since about 1960 there have been many more developments in technology and increases in the possibility of social mobility that have assisted the rise of a very open, new morality. Less than seven decades have thus shown us an extreme of actual moral responses, with the direction clearly pointing toward a more open set of socially approved moral responses to the ever-present problems and temptations of human life.

In the main we think of technology first when we are considering extremes of changing responses by men to their environment. The twentieth century is, in point of fact, the most changing technological era history has yet produced. The year 1900 saw man still dependent upon the horse for much of his power, although the automobile was slowly coming in, and the steamship and steam locomotive were highly developed. Throughout the first seven decades of the century Western man has, not gradually, but quickly, learned to navigate the airways (from a power glider at Kitty Hawk, North Carolina, to the moon and Mars probes in sixty years); learned to sail under the seas and the northern ice cap; learned to build millions of motor cars; to burn diesel fuel in his trains and ships; and, at last, to use nuclear power to light his cities, drive his ships, and subdue his enemies. There is a vast gap, a transcendent leap, between the flimsy autos and gliders of 1900 and the space shots and atomic-powered vessels of today. Technological man has moved from one extreme to another within the first half of the present century.

In view of all this radical change, and the hundreds, even thousands, of equally important and extreme changes that man has brought about in the twentieth century, we should not be surprised to see that man's consciousness—his outlook, attitudes, and morality—has changed radically too.

The three basic ways of responding to the problems of human history—the open, the closed, and the liberal—must be understood, then, against the background of man's vast technological and social changes.

What Is "Wrong" with the Conservative and Radical Responses?

When we attempt to establish a psychological basis for the open or radical and the closed or conservative responses to man's problems, it might seem that we have given them an ultimate justification. Indeed, it would appear from a simple understanding of our discussion to argue that only the liberal pattern of human response (which is a mixture of the two other patterns, strung together by a sense of appropriateness of response to stimuli) is "artificial," cerebral, or learned. Actually, in man, all patterns of response are fundamentally learned—in that the simple psychological and physiological bases of the various patterns are present in all men and the type of pattern that becomes dominant is due to social and "educational" forces. In a real way, in justification of its name, only the liberal type of response is free. The type of person we might call the "compulsive conservative" and the "reacting radical" is not fully free to that degree in which he acts out of psychological conditioning and

habit. What some commentators have called "knee-jerk liberalism" would fall into the same unfree category—although, in the
case of this epithet, it is not liberalism but social radicalism that
is being described.

We may answer our question above, then, with the observation that any pattern of behavior which is compulsive or non-
reflective is wrong in that it is a failure of man to transcend the
emotional dimension by recourse to logical thought.

Compulsive Patterns of Response to Humanity's Problems

At the basis of all compulsive human behavior two conditions
can be discerned: mental laziness (or ignorance) and/or cynicism. A man's lack of free response to a problem or challenge
that confronts him is a sure sign that (1) he doesn't recognize
the problem or understand it, or else misunderstands the real
nature of the problem or the source of the challenge; and/or
(2) he is cynical, i.e., sure that the outcome or resolution of the
problem will not be seriously affected by any effort on his part.
Ignorance is intolerable, of course, since it precludes the full use
of man's powers, but cynicism is an even worse disability since
it has the effect of paralyzing even the intelligent and able.

Both the radical activity of the past beatnik era and that of
many hippies today are marked by ignorance of the full extent
of man's present-day problems and by cynicism about the possibility of any helpful solutions to these problems. It is this
ignorance of useful means for the securing of desirable ends and
the concomitant (and to some degree, resultant) cynicism about
means and ends which lead to the dropout syndrome in modern
American culture. If we do not know how to gain racial har-
mony and international peace and we are entirely skeptical
about any good resolutions to those problems, then dropping out
makes logical sense—from within the framework of the hippie
only, of course.

By the same token, if we are ignorant of the real nature of
the social and international problems of the day, preferring to

believe that student and urban Negro unrest is caused by "Communist agitators" and that the world is threatened by a Communist conspiracy that must be constantly fought, even if in behalf of dictators, then we are apt to be conservative and cynical. Our cynicism grows directly out of our spiritual, historical, and social ignorance, and it compels us to feel that nothing progressive (or very little) needs to be done. Rather, in completely blind cynicism, the conservatives are likely to call for the brutal use of troops on students and the protesting poor. In both cases the compulsion of a radical or conservative response grows out of ignorance and cynicism. As the proverb has it, "There are none so blind as those who will not see."

Some Typical Compulsive Reactions

It is fashionable today to choose up sides and to pick out the weakness of the pattern of response that we happen to reject. For that vast majority of Americans who fall into the middle class (or should we say, rise into it?), the standard group to denounce is the open subculture made up of hippies, students, the new left, and the undifferentiated subgroup that sympathizes with them. For the young and rebellious, as well as for many of their academic servicemen, the standard for denunciation is the middle class. Let us examine some of these typical compulsive responses.

There is, of course, a core of good reasons undergirding a rational decision to become, through decision and response, radical in one's stance in society, or, on the other hand, to become more or less conservative in one's posture. We are not concerned here with those reasons (although we have devoted much space and time in earlier chapters to a discussion of the reasons why many men are radical today), for we want now to underscore the compulsiveness of much human social behavior.

A typical case of compulsive radical behavior would be the hippie who deliberately flaunts existing drug laws (all question of the wisdom of such laws aside) and who retreats into a fantasy world of hallucinations induced by LSD. This passive, dropping-out attitude may be brought back to touch reality only by arrest, severe illness, or sudden accident. Such behavior, not unlike the symbolic retreat to the womb of some kinds of psychotic individuals, is grounded in a contemptuous ignorance and an acidlike cynicism. In his rejection of the middle class's quest for security and recognition, the hippie shows a similar quest (turned inside out) by seeking security in his escape from life's problems and by his attaining recognition as an individual through deviant behavior. The novels of Jack Kerouac (such as *On the Road*[9]) and the records of city hospitals which must treat the "spaced out" hippie when his drugged condition gets him into trouble are our best records of this form of compulsion.

A typical case of the "closed" pattern of response to life's problems that has become compulsive could be modeled on the life-style and public activities and pronouncements of certain Southern politicians. These men have propelled themselves to positions of power and influence through the manipulation of the closed life patterns of many of their constituents (especially their white lower-middle-class and middle-class constituents). These politicians actually magnify the ignorance and cynicism of the people they represent through the shrill use of the mass media and by the identification of real and fancied "threats" to the life pattern of response of their followers. Apparently the activities of these "statesmen" are deeply satisfying—emotionally—to their people, for they are elected again and again, although they may be incapable of that form of political compromise which ensures success for necessary and/or desirable regional projects. Two chief items of response seem to be compulsive in this breed: responses designed "to keep the Negro down," and "to keep the Armed Forces up." In both cases, the compulsiveness of this behavior is abetted (and made more terrible for the nation as a whole) by the addition of rational factors. Both these factors are economic: keeping the Negro down and the military up works to the economic advantage—

over the short run only, to be sure—of the people who support the Senator Claghorn type of politician.

Sometimes we lose patience and feel like condemning the radical militants (and the dropouts), on the one hand, and the reactionary politicians and business leaders, on the other, all to the same perdition. But in our rational moments we must recognize these types of people for what they are—unfree personalities—and learn how to live with them, and to control them, lest we all destroy each other.

Active and Passive Styles of Life on the Left

In searching for a meaning for their own lives that will (or, at least, may) endow the old, eroded Western religious and cultural symbols with new (or the "real, inner") meaning again, the open type of personality, found on the "left hand" of American life, has multiplied itself like a simple organism, by division. Basically, there are the active or new left types of open personalities who are intensely concerned with political, social, and moral issues, on the one hand; and the passive, dropout-prone, drug-use-prone hippie types, on the other.

The active type of open personality is equivalent to the Dostoevskian revolutionary. This action-oriented, highly sensitive type of person feels the mistreatment of the poor, the humiliation and emasculation of the Negro, and the suffering of people in war directly, personally, in his own psyche. A 1968 article describing an interview with a Harvard honor student maintained that 25 percent of the graduating seniors at Harvard were of this general type. These students insisted that they would not take part in the Vietnam war, even if it meant they would have to go to prison for draft evasion or would have to leave the country and flee to Canada.

A very large number of these active, new left types are found in America. Sometimes the conservative opposition (through the press) tries to downgrade their numbers, but we should not make that mistake. The number of people, especially of the current student generation, who are being forced by current problems and the inadequate response of churchly and governmental policies to the solutions of these problems to rebel against the deadness of traditional symbols and patterns of response is growing from year to year. A man or woman must find some meaningfulness—of his or her own—in life, and when the profession of love and concern on the part of society is contradicted by compulsive actions based on selfishness, ignorance, and cynicism, then the person who searches for meaning will search for it outside the present fabric of society. It is this search for meaning (for the adolescent a part of his life goal, searching for a sense of self-identity) that really empowers the massive protests of American students, from Berkeley to Columbia University. It is a similar search for meaningfulness—for some aspect of the reality principle in their studies; for some relevance to their lives and to the problems of the world—that led to the terrible street fighting and the near-anarchy of the French students in Paris, in May, 1968.

The passive life-style on the left is the gentle and rather pathetic attitude and behavior of what the mass media have named "the Flower Children." This passive, retiring, nonviolent life-style is well suited to draw our admiration and, perhaps, our envy in such troubled times. The fatigue which catches up with all of us eventually, both a psychic and a physical fatigue from trying to do so much in what is, for every life, a limited amount of time, makes us feel that dropping out may be a sound idea. And, indeed, it is. Dropping out, withdrawing, pausing to meditate, fleeing the world, seeking out a lonely place to pray—all are ancient, honorable, and healthy "activities." Ours is, perhaps, one of history's few eras that has psychologically "bent us" against the natural rhythm of day and night, winter and summer, work and rest. Although we have so much more leisure time for everybody (not just for the very rich) than any previous era, we have filled up the time with a million activities that militate against the one thing needful—withdrawal from activity for a time so as to gain a better perspective on ourselves and on humanity's problems.

Because the rhythm of advance and withdrawal, of work and rest, has become shattered in the psyches of millions of urbanized Westerners, we are apt material for the missionary work of Hindu gurus and Zen Buddhist adepts. The Maharishi Mahesh Yogi, so popular a few years ago, performed a function for our culture—he reminded us of truths our grandparents (on the farm) knew, but which we have forgotten. As an old Korean once said to me when he saw the field generators set up to supply electricity to our Marine encampment: "You have forgotten the truth about time. You have broken the cycle of work and rest. You have lit an imaginary sun and raped the night, stealing away her healing powers. If your tomorrow is not good, it will only be because you robbed tomorrow tonight for the sake of today." The example of the passive hippie and of the Indian holy man is wholly good in this regard. Both of them alike stand as living symbols of a better style of life we all need to follow.

But withdrawal is only one phase of the style of man's life. Before withdrawal there must be work and accomplishment. He who does not exercise himself hardly rests well. This is the insight that the passive hippie has forgotten. Discipline must precede pleasure, and activity comes before withdrawal.

The life of Henry David Thoreau (1817–1862) is illustrative of the argument advanced above. Thoreau is often cited as a folk hero by both the active and the passive wings of the hippies and also by the activistic new left. Thoreau is often cited for his withdrawal from society; most often remembered for his retreat to Walden Pond.[10] His life has become a sort of symbol and inspiration to the dropouts who flock to "hippie hangouts." However, Thoreau, like most great thinkers, was a man of many parts. He was also active in his opposition to governmental policies and social practices he considered unjust. Thoreau went to jail for refusal to pay taxes to a government that had a Fugitive Slave Act. He preached by his presence in prison more eloquently than Ralph Waldo Emerson who limited his protest to words.

We should also recognize that Mahatma Gandhi and Martin Luther King, Jr., two great social and spiritual leaders of the twentieth century who were very much influenced by Thoreau's nonviolent, passive resistance, were also men of action as well as of withdrawal. There should be no surprise in considering that these two men of peace, drunk as it were with the Divine Spirit, were both cut down by the guns of a fanatical opposition —an opposition based on ignorance and cynicism. Many times our enemies will let us alone when all we do is talk, but their attitude becomes more aggressive when we begin to do something. Gandhi's many imprisonments, his fasts, and speeches finally led India to independence. When that nation began to constitute itself as a Hindu republic, then the murder of Gandhi —in revenge—took place. In the case of Martin Luther King, Jr., his work in Chicago and, above all, his planned poor people's march on Washington and his involvement in the sanitation workers' fight in Memphis made his martyrdom inevitable. But despite this danger, the bearer of the new mentality must be willing to put his thought into action, his belief into the raw stuff of everyday life.

Hippies and Hawks

Almost like living parodies of the two types of extreme response to human problems which we characterized above as the open and the closed patterns of response are the "peaceniks" or pacifistic hippies and other protestors against the draft and the war in Vietnam (open) and the modern "war hawks"[11] (closed) who run the gamut from those who want the United States to stay militarily supreme in the world to some politicians and citizens who want to drop atomic bombs on all our enemies, real or imaginary. Both these groups—and unfortunately the closed group seems by far the larger, although it is daily losing ground—are striving, through their political (and apolitical) activities to give new, or regenerated, meanings to the symbols of nation, race, brotherhood, and culture that have lost much of their power to move men to self-transcendence during the course of the twentieth century.

In this context, where we have examined the open and closed manners in which men respond to the world's problems, we can see that those left-wing persons who simply drop out are really an inauthentic left. The dropouts who turn to drugs or to communes for safety from life are actually new bohemians, interested only in hedonism or self-pleasure, and so are not genuine exemplars of the new mentality. While the activistic left faces up to the excesses of the reactionary right and the hawks in power (with excesses of their own), the new bohemians sit out the struggle in comfort. The dropouts may, indeed, be doing a highly technologized society a real service by exploring and opening up new forms of life-fulfilling creative leisure, but they are not taking part in the struggle for answers to the political problems of our time. The fact remains that those who do not participate in the problems of their own day sacrifice much of what it means to be a human being.

Civil Rights Activists and Segregationists

The open-minded, open-handed response to the endemic racial problems of Western society (especially in America, but also in Great Britain) on the part of the civil rights activists is well known. Conversely, the closed-minded, closed-handed pattern of response to this crisis of human social cooperation by those who are admittedly or unadmittedly segregationists, is also well known. However, this problem, because of its age, size, and complexity, reveals a further bifurcation of each group. On the left, there are some open-response civil rights types who struggle to reform our society, but there are many more closed-response types (at least closed for all practical purposes) who recognize the justice in the movement but who will not involve themselves in the activities that must be carried out if the problem is to be solved. Similarly, within the right-wing camp there are only a few very active (and very dangerous) persons who overtly perform acts designed either to preserve the *status quo* or to bring about a reactionary shift in social standards. These activists, mainly psychotic and/or ignorant men, are at least positive in their response to current conditions as they try to do something to effect a change. The vast majority of people on the right (including most of the middle class and much of the upper class) are really passive, negative, i.e., show a closed pattern of response to the racial crisis. They form the great weight of intolerance and "white racism" which the President's Commission (1968) declared was the chief roadblock to racial peace.[12]

Here we have a clear case of the effect that a cadre or cell group (in economic terms, the "margin" has upon the total group. All our citizens could be polled and distributed among the various groups that make up the political and social spectrum, but (since they are already so divided, in their own minds) it would make no real difference, for it is the activistic minority in each camp that determines the direction each camp (and the nation which is composed of "camps") will take in the future. From this we can conclude that the task of refilling the traditional but eroded symbols of Western culture will be done (if it is done at all) by these activistic minorities. It is the passive majorities who are powerless, not the active minorities, since the passive hand over their powers—through default—to those with the courage to exercise that power.

Eastern Religions and the Younger Generation

The colorful, exotic religions and philosophies of Asia have exercised a fascination on the Western mind since the return of Marco Polo from Cathay. For centuries, however, little was known of the teachings of these systems of thought, since attention was directed chiefly to the rituals, art, and social customs of their adherents. There were exceptions, to be sure, but until the nineteenth century there was not much scientific study of

Eastern thought. In America, Ralph Waldo Emerson brought the influence of the Vedantic writings into the transcendentalist movement. In Europe, Arthur Schopenhauer felt that the Eastern attitude toward death and life was superior to the Western attitude. During the course of the nineteenth century, the sciences of philology, anthropology, and the history of religions were developed, making the understanding of Eastern thought at least theoretically possible.

The Eastern world became more and more important to European countries, and to the United States, which was beginning to feel its status as a Pacific power during the late nineteenth and early twentieth centuries. In the course of the last seven decades Asia has become, perhaps, America's chief interest and certainly its number-one problem.

The involvement of America in Asian affairs goes back many years to the clipper-ship trade with China and the whaling expeditions of New Englanders to the Pacific. As early as 1898, America secured a territorial foothold in the area, taking over the vast Philippine Islands chain and the island of Guam from defeated Spain. Our interest in the East was symbolized by our determined policy of maintaining an "open door" in China.

Many Asiatics came to America; Chinese laborers by the thousands came to California in the nineteenth century as a source of cheap labor for the railroads that were being built everywhere. Thousands more of Filipinos, Japanese, and Koreans came to work in the vegetable fields of California. Only the immigration acts passed by Congress after World War I stopped this inflow from the East. Large "Chinatowns" sprang up in San Francisco, Chicago, New York, and elsewhere across the United States. The "inoculation sites" were established; from this point on, the Eastern religions would be here, ever-attractive, exotic, ready to hand for study and appreciation.

The terrible island battles of World War II cemented American interest in the East. Several things grew out of that war. One interest was America's continuing involvement with Japan, which has grown to be an Asian counterpart of Western society.

Another factor was America's recognition that she is preeminently a Pacific power, and that she must police and guard that vast area of the world.

It is not only America's political background that has led to acquaintance with and acceptance of many elements of the Eastern religions by young people today. To the secular reasons we must add ecclesiastical failure. After World War II, Christianity had a wonderful opportunity to serve mankind—and its own missionary purposes—by bringing a moral and spiritual framework to the lives of millions who were in spiritual shock and a moral vacuum. Christianity failed to serve man or its own purposes, first in Europe, then in Japan,[13] and later in America. The "return to religion" of the late 1940's and the 1950's soon shifted to a growing indifference to Christianity, which, of late, has begun to be a negative feeling toward the church in general. It is because of the failure of Christianity to become and remain relevant to men's needs today that the younger generation is increasingly turning to the mysticism and meditation of the Eastern religions.

The chief Eastern movements that have affected American young people since World War II have been Zen Buddhism and Hindu Vedanta philosophy. The major spokesman for Zen among the beats of a decade ago, who now speaks equally well for the hippie generation, is Alan W. Watts, of California. Watts is the dean of the American Academy of Asian Studies at San Francisco and the author of a number of works on Buddhism and Christianity. The concept of Zen meditation, the techniques of Zen designed to bring enlightenment (*satori*), and the associated rituals of Zen such as the tea ceremony and the weaponless arts of self-defense have become an important part of American culture in recent years. It is ironic that while acquaintance with Zen Buddhism (a Japanese sect) is making more and more American young people contemplative, the Southeast Asian variants of Buddhism are becoming more politically active and militant.

The Influence of Hinduism

While there are a number of Hindu gurus, or religious teachers, active in Europe and America today, the most famous and successful in the modern period was the mentor of the Beatles and the Beachboys, the Maharishi Mahesh Yogi or "the Great Sage." The Maharishi, an exotic figure, to be sure, with a thin, pedantic voice, was a man of attractive personality and great sincerity. Although he is no longer in the public eye, his career in America can be taken as a symbol of the influence of Hinduism on the new mentality. The Maharishi apparently accomplished a great deal after coming to the United States from France in 1959. There is a world governor, Charles F. Lutes, who heads the International Spiritual Regeneration Movement, the organizational embodiment of the Maharishi's message.[14] The Maharishi's words circulated widely in a paperback book, *Meditations of Maharishi Mahesh Yogi.*[15] His message was very Hindu, very much the essential Vedantic philosophy that has been directed to the West by various Indian groups throughout the twentieth century. This is by no means a harsh criticism of the Maharishi's message, for, to an objective mind, there is much that is noble in his teaching. Its chief drawbacks are the traditional Hindu elements that justify a kind of spiritual caste system[16] and the emphasis on karma as the law of cosmic retribution, by which even the suffering of children is justified on the basis of supposed evil deeds in previous existences.[17] Undoubtedly it is these two basic Hindu ideas (caste and karma)—which are actually based on the same doctrine, the concept of spiritual cause and effect, or karma—that prevented Vedanta from being more than an interesting possibility for Western man. In the last analysis, the idea of karma and the practice of caste is demonic, destructive of the inner integrity of man and the outer cohesiveness of brotherhood.

In the summer of 1968 the Maharishi, after receiving wide publicity and attracting much attention from young and old alike, announced that his mission to the West had failed. He returned to India and went into seclusion at his retreat center, where he remains still.

Still Searching for a New Meaning of Old Symbols

The messages of Zen[18] and Vedanta are of unquestioned interest to many of the bearers of the new mentality. This by no means implies that many of them have or will accept an Eastern form of religion when they have rejected so much of Western religion. To the contrary, the teachings of these liberalized forms of Eastern faith are of interest to the bearers of the new mode of thought precisely to the extent that Zen and Vedanta offer to men a form of feeling and human sensibility that seems lacking in so much of Western religion and philosophy. It is this personal sensitivity and the emphasis on positive spiritual elements that attracts Western man. The ideal of a kingdom where men will find a peace for their own lives and the power to live in peace with one another attracts the bearers of the new mentality, as it attracts all spiritually sensitive and intelligent men. It is the mark of institutionalized Western Christianity's greatest failure that the sons and daughters of Western culture must look to Hinduism and Buddhism for the very ideal and the very style of life (the Christlike style) that is the historic foundation of European self-consciousness. *We must observe that God may not so much be dead as dead in any Western cultural expression.*

Since the springs of the Spirit seem dried up in the West, the thirsty spirit then turns to the strange but still-flowing streams of the East. But it is important to note that the water flowing there, the symbols operative there, are similar to the symbols of the West. Therefore, such a cultural turnabout is not the answer to the quest for new symbols or for new meanings for old symbols. Ultimately, it will become clear to the young that, beneath the exotic surface, the symbols of Zen and Vedanta have the same weaknesses, and many of the same strengths, that the symbols of Judaism and Christianity do. When that awakening comes even the hippies will come to feel that God is dead if we have not, in the meantime, revitalized the symbols of Western culture. The interest in Eastern religions, then, is not an answer to Western problems, but, at best, is only a period of grace during which Western Judaism and Christianity had best work diligently. A night of spiritual meaninglessness is possible, in the not too remote future, when no religious symbol will be either appropriate or available. When and if that happens we may well experience the end of man, for man is an incurably religious and idealistic creature who requires meaning for life even more than he requires water and food. Whenever the symbol of God dies the men who were dependent upon that God die too.

VI

Revitalization
of Traditional Symbols

*T*HE late novelist, playwright, and existentialist philosopher
Albert Camus, writing in *The Rebel*,[1] declared that rebellion
is not chaos, not anarchy, not even the opposite of order and
moral codes, but is precisely a response of outrage at the injustice so fundamentally involved in the structures of human life-
world. Genuine rebellion recognizes the need for limits, limits
which enable us to understand the world in which we find ourselves and limits which structure our involvements with each
other. For the existentialist, "man is a project." Man is incom-
plete, ever seeking to make himself out of nothing into something. If man is, indeed, a project, striving to perfect himself,
then he needs a rule of thumb, a guide, some limits within which
to grow, lest he lose himself—bled away in a million meaningless encounters—before his project is completed.

The conception of man as a project, of man creating himself,
is basic to European (especially French) existentialism. In Jean-
Paul Sartre the idea of man's self-project is spelled out in meta-
physical terms in *Being and Nothingness, Existential Psychoanalysis*,[2] and in the little essay "Existentialism Is a Humanism."[3]

Essentially, Sartre declares that man is a passion, which may
be Sartre's interpretation of Husserl's doctrine that man's basic
being is his consciousness-of-the-world of meaning, or man's in-
tentionality.[4] Man, who is precisely this useless passion (Sartre
declares the passion man is, to be, ultimately, useless), is thus

a project who creates himself. For Sartre, man's passion and his projects are attempts to become God. By man's drive to become God, Sartre means, essentially, that man drives himself on through the nexus of interrelations and tasks we call social life, ever seeking the meaning of his very being. "God" means that whole in which meaning and being coincide. Throughout his existence, however, man never finds the full meaning of his life —such meaning sometimes seems a fiction, and constantly eludes man.

The Meaning of Meaning

Whatever is this meaning man seems to seek? Why did human creatures ever raise the question of meaning? What is the meaning of meaning? This line of questioning, rather than a waste of time, is the most serious task man can set for himself. Man must be at least partially a philosopher if he is ever to make sense of himself.

"Meaning" has three major dictionary definitions, none of which fit the human situation we have described above. (1) Meaning can be the symptom of some event; (2) meaning may be the purpose of an action; and (3) meaning is that which is referred to by a word or symbol.[5] In addition, there is the semantic conception of meaning, such as that used to construct dictionaries, in which two types of "meaning" are distinguished: the denotative and the connotative. Unfortunately, a great segment of modern philosophy has gotten carried away by searching for meaning in language and words, forgetting the poor creature who invents and uses language—man—who is all the while using that language to ask himself about the meaning of his life.

While the meaning that man seeks includes some conception of purpose ("What is it all for?") there is more to the meaning (real or imaginary) that man desires. At a minimum, man wants a meaning that includes an intrinsic good—happiness and satisfaction in themselves, apart from any furtherance of a larger purpose. Man above all wants to feel, to experience his own meaning here and now. After that self-fulfillment has been achieved, then man turns to concepts of the future in which his meanings will be seen to fulfill certain purposes.

Radical Anthropology

There is a symbol available to modern-day man that is sufficiently available to him and appropriate to the tasks of self-integration and community creation that are necessary for man to accomplish if he is to continue his progress forward as a full human being. This symbol is a radical anthropology that stresses the divine element in man. This is not a materialistic symbol, not a reduction of theology to anthropology, but rather a re-evaluation of man by use of the traditional symbols used to interpret the Christ event. The materials for the discovery and appropriation of this symbol are readily available to us in the traditions of the Christian religion. They are particularly available to us in the writings of Pierre Teilhard de Chardin and Nicolas Berdyaev. Berdyaev, mystical existentialist and reinterpreter of the Eastern Orthodox tradition, has written beautifully of the participation of man, the creative creature, in the life of the Divine. Man is, Berdyaev holds, the spiritual center of the universe, although he is only, physically, an incidental creature among other creatures. Man's preeminent position in the nexus of things is due solely to his mental and spiritual constitution. It is through man that the universe knows itself and creates form out of chaos.

The Christ event, in which Jesus made the essence of divinity, its creativity and loving concern, known through his utter humility and emptying of himself in loving identification of himself with the poor and the suffering, has brought God into the world of history as well as elevating manhood into the dimension of the Divine. Manhood, humanity, human beingness

(*Dasein*) is thus a fit subject/object for worship since the acceptance of Jesus as the Christ by the early Christians. The belief that Jesus is the Christ is confirmed by the power that has flowed from the symbols connected with Jesus to his followers for almost two thousand years. The confirmation of Jesus' Christhood, in my opinion, is his acceptance as the Christ (the God revealer) by millions upon millions of men for over nineteen hundred years and the effect, in transformed styles of living, his symbol has had upon so many of these men. The confirmation of Christ lies in the changed lives of Christian believers.

The availability and appropriateness of a symbol of the divine depths of humanity is confirmed also by its connection with the responsible humanity called for by the humanistic existentialism of Albert Camus. The symbol we propose, one that underscores the Jesus-like quality of every human being, thus fits the existential exhortation that we see man as a project (to become more Jesus-like), love as the agency and instrument of his project, and the temporal amelioration of hate, war, torture, prejudice, ignorance, disease, and self-estrangement as the goal. Berdyaev's theological stress on man's creativity as the sign of his participation in divinity thus undergirds for us the humanism of Camus.

Phenomenology as the Method for Measuring Our Life Space[6]

Obviously, the methods of traditional theology are too narrow to deal with the problem of the death of religious and cultural symbols and their revitalization. Not so obviously, but just as surely, the methods of anthropology, sociology, and psychology (and even psychoanalysis) are inadequate to this task. The various methods of language analysis formed by the modern schools of philosophy since the pioneering work of G. E. Moore and Bertrand Russell also fail to meet the conditions required for the development of a radical anthropology as a reevaluation of Christian symbolism. Only a method that goes to the depths of the process of life itself, beyond the most general forms of every human experience, can begin to glimpse obliquely the truth about the functioning of such religious symbols. Such a prephilosophical method is the phenomenology of Husserl.

Phenomenology is a radical empiricism and is concerned with the fullness of experience in its total, concrete, existential density. There are, according to Husserl, many kinds of life-worlds, and therefore many kinds of experiential-structures of life-experiencing-the-world. There is the impersonal (or pre-personal), public, taken-for-granted world within whose horizon we live our "natural" lives. There are more humanly and socially structured worlds of intersubjectivity, of language, of expression, and all forms of communication. There are the still more personally structured worlds of various social groups, cultures, historical epochs. Finally there are those incommunicable or imperfectly communicable worlds of private experience which each man possesses as his own. For this reason the phenomenological elucidation of experience must be carried out on many different levels, as yet only very imperfectly distinguished. Phenomenology is thus a transcendentalism of a very special type, and it is precisely because of this richness and flexibility that it has already been able to illuminate in many ways the theoretical foundations of depth-psychology, psychoanalysis, social studies, and other disciplines. There is not, in principle, any *phenomenon* (in the phenomenological sense of this term), or any area of human experience—from the universally valid categorical judgments of reflexive consciousness to the hidden pre-logical and pre-conceptual structures of the individual and collective subconscious—that falls outside the competence of phenomenological analysis. Like pragmatism, it is open to all kinds of human experience.[7]

With the phenomenological method, we may be able to describe to ourselves the meaning of our religious (or areligious) experiences, so that we might recognize what kind of symbols (and our possible participation in such symbols) may be present now and which possess the quality of creativity for the future.

Beyond Eastern Mysticism and Traditional Western Doctrines

Berdyaev has written:

Materialistic Europe, having betrayed its faith of Christ, finds it easy to accept Eastern spiritualism, and reconciles it with its science. It is a strange and terrible thing to say, but Christianity is becoming more foreign and less acceptable to the modern mind of Christian Europe than Buddhism.[8]

What he has written is as true of the United States as it is of Europe. Our earlier discussion of the fascination of the younger generation with the Vedas, the Hindu gurus, and Zen Buddhism should well illustrate the pertinence of Berdyaev's remarks. Yet, conversation with ordinary people, including the "ordinary" members of the younger generation who bear the new mentality, reveals the fact that the Jesus recorded in the Gospels (shorn of his mythological attributes, to be sure) is universally admired. One wonders—frankly, with no prejudice because of any religious commitment to Christianity—why Buddha or a Hindu sage would be preferred as a source of inspiration over Jesus. Everything that the Western mind admires in the records of Buddha and the Hindu mahatmas it admires because the lives of those good men remind it of the common stories of Jesus.

We must remember this order of knowledge: first the Western mind hears something about Jesus, then it learns of Buddha and the Hindu sages. Jesus is the model by which all the other good men of history are measured by Western men. We may well ask why this is the case, because the most obvious reason for this veneration of Jesus, religious faith in the older sense, is no longer the factor it once was. Actually, Jesus as a person, as a man, a human figure and exemplar, increases in stature during periods of rationalism and humanism. The reason for this appreciation of the human Jesus by men with little supernaturally oriented religious faith is that Jesus is a figure of *man the creator of values,* man the bearer of reason, even of man the bearer of

uncommon "common sense." Jesus is meaningful, precisely because Jesus is a genuine human being. Man is meaning, the primordial, the only meaning in the universe of chance we inhabit.
Man is the maker and the bearer of meaning, and Jesus is one
of the most creative makers of meaning and value the world
has ever known. Perhaps Jesus is the uniquely creative meaning
maker of all human history just because of the magnificent manner in which he bore the meaning he made and exemplified the
values he uncovered in man's social world.[9]

Jesus has been called "the eternal contemporary" by religious
thinkers in many times and places. To a much greater extent
than is generally the case, this religious assertion seems to me to
be true. Søren Kierkegaard, in his passionately individual way,
even asserted that the believer in Jesus Christ becomes contem-
poraneous with Christ. Whatever may be our theological or
philosophical assessment of the experience—and we believe
phenomenology may aid us in describing and so understanding
this experience of participation in fellowship with the Spirit of
Jesus—we cannot gainsay it. Let us make no mistake about the
actual religious situation in the West: the church is dying, if
not yet dead; yet the symbol of Jesus as a model (*Vorbild*,
exemplar, guide, pattern for imitation) is as attractive and
power-giving as it has ever been. Every atheist that ever lived,
who was worth his atheism, has admired Jesus. Friedrich
Nietzsche tried to despise Jesus and found that he could not.[10]
Karl Marx turned Ludwig Feuerbach's profound rendering of
theology as anthropology upside down[11]—as he also claimed to
have treated Hegel—and on the basis of this misreading of his
philosophical influences declared religion to be the opiate of the
masses—and still, Marx could not despise the Jesus of the
Gospels who is presented as the friend of the poor and the healer
of the sick, the fearful, and the alienated. No humanist, no
naturalist, indeed few men who have left the church out of a
sense of moral outrage over the hypocrisy and reactionary attitude of clergy and churchmen, have done so out of a revulsion
against Jesus. Indeed, many have become humanists, or at least

have left the church, precisely because of the veneration they came to feel for the Jesus of the Gospels and because of the split between the actions of the Jesus of the New Testament and the actions of the people called Christians. The medieval Catholic Church was perhaps wise to try to limit the reading of the Bible to the few. The symbol of Jesus that still exercises power in the Western world is, in a sense, the same symbol that has been influential in Europe and America since the Enlightenment. It is the symbol of the man who put others before himself and taught men to do the same.

Offenses in the Jesus Symbol

There are one or two episodes in the Gospel records of Jesus that have offended the liberal mind in the past and continue to do so in the present. Our only defense against this offense is the observation that these episodes are either misinterpretations, later accretions to the record, or, at a minimum, are not necessary parts of the record and image of the Biblical Jesus. The first of these offensive episodes revolves around the reported words of Jesus to the effect that there will always be wars and rumors of wars (Mark 13:7–8). The liberal mind has never accepted that outlook, and the new mentality reflects its liberal heritage in this regard. In fact, the liberal outlook is correct and much more Jesus-like than these very words put into Jesus' mouth by the evangelist-editor. The new mentality rejects war and the necessity for war, and on this score is far more genuinely religious—and Christian—than the traditional churches. The second episode revolves around the reported words of Jesus to the effect that the poor will be with us always (John 12:4–8). This quietistic[12] outlook has been rejected by the nineteenth- and twentieth-century liberal mind, and is strongly rejected by the bearers of the new mentality. In this rejection the new mentality is right—and far more like the Jesus of the average Gospel pericope[13] than is the Jesus who is represented as saying this about the poor. Both of these sayings ought to be banned from any future theology or Christology—or Jesus-like anthropology —or at least completely reinterpreted.

The most offensive episode revolves around Jesus' calling the Gentile woman a dog in the healing account in Mark 7:25–30. I once had an Eastern European colleague who had suffered much in World War II, even to the extent of internment in a concentration camp. This European intellectual had been reared as an Eastern Orthodox Christian and knew much of the ritual and theology of Christianity, but he refused to attend either the Greek Orthodox or any other church in this country, because of a deep-seated feeling of offense against Jesus which he had gained from his own study of the New Testament, specifically the story in Mark 7:25–30. This sensitive, very liberal man thought that the reference to the Gentile woman as a dog in the Mark pericope disqualified Jesus as a moral exemplar. It took a good deal of discussion to convince him (1) that Jesus did help the woman (since the only true test of one's morality is the change in one's life when he is called to do good and cease doing evil), and (2) that the term "dog" was a Jewish term of derision for non-Jewish pagans that had become a usual, everyday term among Jews. Jesus' use of the term—even if we could be sure that we have something like the real gist of Jesus' conversation, which we cannot be sure of—means no more, on this interpretation, than that Jesus used the terms and phrases typical of his nation and class. The traditional apologetic for the liberal sensitivity to this Gospel passage is that Jesus was testing the Gentile woman's faith. This interpretation becomes ridiculous when we consider (1) that Jesus many times helped people without testing their faith (one woman was healed by only touching his robe, others were healed "at a distance," according to the Gospels), and (2) that if Jesus was testing this woman because she was a Gentile, then Jesus really was prejudiced. Fortunately, neither this nor any other traditional interpretation is needed; this passage strikes me as nongenuine. It is not convincing as a report of the Jesus we usually meet in the Gospels, nor is it particularly edifying. In short, it is a miracle story. We would do well to forget it.

There Is No Road to Dasein, Dasein *Is the Road*

The built-in failure factor of all philosophers and theologians (this philosopher very definitely included) is their predilection for preliminary statement; their weakness for overqualification; their dependence upon prolegomena, antilegomena, and heavy footnotes. What we must allow ourselves to do here is to go straight to the heart of the matter and say that what the human race must have if it is to endure as a species is a living, concrete symbol. It does not need a totem of a god; no animal or technical object is elevated enough for man's deepest needs, for only man himself is close enough and high enough for man to worship. In the final analysis, man is the meaning of life. Without theological "horns and teeth" (as Luther would have said), this is the meaning of Christ. Christ is God to man as he is man to God.

There is no way to tell people how to be human. There can be no genuine how-to-do-it books on philosophy, theology, morality, or religion. One is either fully human or deficiently human. One has achieved *Dasein* either fully already, or not yet, or never will. There is no "way" to become human. One already is potentially human; one must only will his humanity to grow. Our humanity is our meaning; our meaning is the way we are to follow. And whether we agree with this or not makes no difference, for this is simply the way things are. There is no road to *Dasein,* to real, human, sensitive, constructive, "authentic" existence. *Dasein* is the road. Merely to allow ourselves to be human —to feel, to love, to respond, to be curious, to forgive—is to achieve the fullness of *Dasein.* If we once reach the level of this fullness of humanity, we will have all that we require for meaning in life; while, if we miss this state of *Dasein,* we will go through life empty though we may possess the ability to secure every pleasure known to man. Jesus knew the fullness of *Dasein* and so could not be finally defeated even by a criminal's rejection and execution. Socrates knew what full humanity meant and so filled up his life wtih meaning, a meaning that no false charges or unjust sentence could erase. Paul knew *Dasein* and hence could declare:

For my deep desire and hope is that I shall never fail my duty, but that at all times, and especially right now, I shall be full of courage, so that with my whole self I shall bring honor to Christ, whether I live or die. For what is life? To me, it is Christ! Death, then, will be gain.[14]

Paul had achieved true *Dasein*, a spiritualized anthropology, a divinization of human life—and he was consequently freed from anxiety, the fear of loss of status, from unnecessary (and therefore pseudo) desires, and from the fear of death itself. He was a man in all the fullness man can attain. For him, life was Christ; life was divine humanity.

Becoming Fully Human

Our question regarding an absolute anthropocentricism must be, What are the dimensions of such an anthropology? Again, we might phrase the question, What are the dimensions of "a measured space" (a vision of man) within man that will enable man to preserve his life and the continuity of life's processes without blighting freedom's creative glibness and disorder, its characteristic lack of concern for absolutes? *The inner aim of the new mentality is a drive to discover just such a measured space of creative possibilities and healthy limits.* Such limits are not limits to be imposed from without a man, but freely elected limits measured from within. As of now we see only through a glass darkly, and we have no clear idea of the conjunction of the elements of freedom and discipline that is necessary for the creation of an ethic to supplement our new anthropology. We, as yet, can only hypothesize that the life-style of the young men and women who are bearers of the new mentality will be closer to that of the hippies and other protesting groups of today than to that of the secure, and yet anxious, middle class.

Radical Christocentrism

Plato says in *The Laws,* "No soul can maintain the fight against injustice without a spirit of righteous indignation." We have remarked several times earlier about the motive power of moral outrage as it is operational in the bearers of the new mentality, and we here want to suggest that this moral indignation, channeled and directed against the real problems of our life together, will probably form the dimensions of what we term "a measured space." Some of these genuine problem areas are the relationships including intra- and inner relationships between the male and female elements within each human being and the relationships of male and female beings in society. Others of these problems involve the relationships of men to the means of production and to natural and manufactured products. The works of Carl Gustav Jung may help us here.[15]

We offer the insights of Jung as possible aids to the creation of a new theology (really a spiritualized anthropology) because of his profound teaching, shared by Paul Tillich, that historical mankind will never "outgrow" religion or the influence of religiously oriented symbols upon it. With Luther, Jung along with Tillich can say, "Man will ever have either the true God or an idol." Secularity does not mean atheism. Man qua man is a being with meaning, and the meaning of his being is the subject matter of religion.

Perhaps this view, that religion involves man's reflection upon and reaction to the meaning of his being, may seem a finite or naturalistic conception of religion to some. But no kind of materialism, no effort at reduction of religion to psychological categories alone, is intended here. By what other standards would you judge man or religion than by the meaning of man's life? Any theory of religion that leaves it "hanging in the air" above man's head and heart, without a point of contact is no religion—

or faith—at all. Rather, it is empty, prephilosophical speculation, no matter how pious it may be in intentions or words.
Certainly, no hypothesis of the status of religion and no theology
that attempts to define religion apart from man is Christian, for
Christianity is that religion which involves belief in the God-
man.

Here is where our interpretation of the new theology that
proclaims the death of God as a new, absolutized anthropology
connects with the older liberalism. The new theology, seen in
the works of Altizer, Hamilton, and van Buren as well as in the
writings and teachings of the hosts of less well known radical
thinkers, is radically Christocentric. For too long men have forgotten that Christocentric means anthropocentric. The Christ
is Jesus, a man born in Judea two thousand years ago. The very
concept of a Christ means a man approved by and appointed
by God. It is not the stress on the concrete, full humanity of
Jesus Christ that the historic church has declared heretical, but
the docetic,[16] Gnostic[17] interpretation of Jesus as less than a full
human being. For all too long Jesus as *Vorbild,* as image, model,
and pattern, has been made unavailable to most men and women
by the unfortunate—but overt—presentation of Jesus in a docetic manner throughout much of Christian history. Now we must
recover the genuine meaning of Jesus as the Christ—as true man
—man as he is in the achievement of his fullest meaning. Only
when we have recovered the meaning of Jesus as man will we
ever be able to seriously work on the general conception of God.

"Imitatio Christi"

The whole idea of the imitation of Christ is as old as Christianity,[18] and has an impressive history of deepening and development throughout the Middle Ages and again in modern times.
However, in the twentieth century, under the influence of the
neo-orthodox rejection of liberal theology (which stressed the
imitation of Jesus), the idea that imitation of Jesus Christ is a
live option for modern Christians has fallen into disrepute.

It is this "cloud" of neo-orthodox criticism that we must dispel. For, while it seems reasonable to hold that no one can perfectly imitate Jesus Christ, it is unreasonable to suggest that such a perfect imitation (the kind of quest for perfection that drove, and now drives, men and women into the monastery and the convent) is necessary. In any event it seems totally unnecessary to conclude that because a perfect imitation of Jesus is impossible men should not attempt to imitate him as far as is possible. We certainly recommend no more than that here. "To dream the impossible dream," to stretch ourselves to reach an unreachable goal, to venerate an unapproachable ideal, are all normal components of the human urge for self-transcendence. William James, with his warm pragmatism,[19] should be our counselor here, not the colder John Dewey. "A man's reach should exceed his grasp, Or what's a heaven for?"[20] is as profound a statement today as it was when Robert Browning first wrote it. The sounds that the sensitive can hear coming from the silence of men and women who bear the new mentality indicate that these concerned human beings are looking for an ideal of human self-realization like Jesus Christ. In their search for a new sense of human self-transcendence, a pertinent and appropriate presentation of the fully-human Jesus would probably be well received. The fact that other moral exemplars like Buddha and the Hindu gurus, who show Christlike traits, are well received by many today would seem to indicate that there is a ready audience waiting to hear about one whose self-transcendence revealed itself in his positive, loving relationships with other human beings. If Jesus is not as popular with the bearers of the new mentality as Buddha or the gurus, it is the fault of the church and the Christians, not of the "new ones" in our society.

The Gospel and Radical Theology

It may well be too late for any form of Christianity to re-establish a meaningful set of symbols that can integrate and inform Western culture. If this is indeed the case, then all is up not only with the Christian religion but with the West—as a civilization—itself. No culture has survived the death of its basic philosophy and theology, although philosophies and theologies have survived the deaths of the cultures that produced them, in transformed modes (ancient Israel, ancient Greece, Rome). However, it does not seem likely that any form of Christianity will survive the transformation of the West in the future unless its own foundations are put in order. When we look about us for signs of an effort to reestablish the Christian symbols on a firmer foundation, we are struck by the fact that only in the radical movement are men concerned with a search for a newer, more meaningful interpretation of Christian symbols.

Two such possible symbols have been suggested by radical theologians: the Spirit-Christ who is "seen in every human face,"[21] and the "man for others." Both of these symbols are based on the Gospel records of Jesus Christ, of course, and both are not completely new suggestions. The Spirit-Christ seen in the lives of every personality was spoken of by the mystics, by Luther ("Be a little Christ to your neighbor"), and by Gerard Manley Hopkins in his poems.[22] The "man for others" idea is simply a Bonhoeffer phrase for the liberal idea of "following in His steps" that grew out of the developing social gospel movement. We now suggest a further development of the Christ symbol in which elements of both the Spirit-Christ and the "man for others" symbols are combined. Such an emphasis would be a Christ mysticism with a strong element of social activism.

Christ Mysticism: "The Man in Everyman"

An absolute anthropocentricism would seem to be the most fruitful doctrine for contemporary theology to attempt to develop, since the modern mentality is absolutely man-centered. Man—his "nature," his genesis, his prospects and his problems —forms the core of concern of every thinking human being today. By reinterpreting Jesus Christ as the symbol of a healthy humanity we may find it possible to bring men not just to

"Christianity," but, more importantly, to themselves; to their senses and to their unconscious feelings about themselves and others. Such a theological strategy is not really a novel reinterpretation, because Jesus was early understood by the orthodox tradition, as seen in Paul (Rom. 5:12–21) and Irenaeus,[23] as "the New Adam" who "recapitulated" or corrected the historical errors of mankind and opened up a way to a new humanity.

The coincidence of the ancient doctrine of "doing it all over" or recapitulation, the liberal idea of Jesus as moral and spiritual model, and the traditional piety of the imitation of Christ—all cast into the radical evaluation of Jesus as the "man for others" —may well be the symbol of reintegration and reconciliation that Western man needs if he is to rebuild his society. Surely this is a symbol that is possible to recover from the historical tradition and to refurbish with the knowledge that man has gained about psychological and sociological processes.

Jesus: The New Adam—the Man in Man

We must develop a method of expression that will enable us to deal rationally with religious—or mystical—experience. We must base our spiritualized—or absolutized—anthropocentricism upon our apperception of (in Whiteheadian terms, our "prehension" of) the basic and noble qualities we call humane in our species. It is precisely these humane qualities of love, loyalty, courage, hope, and the constructive desires that we may refer to as modifications of animal nature which indicate the presence of Spirit—or Christ—in man. That which is most human in us is most Christlike. Jesus Christ, as model and as inspiration, is the man in our manhood; the human in our humanity. Thomas J. J. Altizer has written of "the Christ we see in every human face." And the Christ is there—in every mark and activity of dignity and integrity that characterizes the human species. The failures among us, and the failure in every one of us, do not obviate our belief. In spite of selfishness and depravity, the essentially human endures throughout man's generations, and these enduring qualities of good and worth indicate Christ's Spirit.

Adolf Deissmann, in his classic work, *Paul: A Study in Social and Religious History*,[24] argues for the necessity of Christ mysticism in Christian piety. By "Christ mysticism" Deissmann meant —and we mean here—a devotion to Jesus Christ which believes that death was not able to destroy his Spirit; that the living presence of Jesus Christ is now liberated from the limitations of a single human life, and is now scattered (spread out) across all the world in everything that lives, in all that exists, as the value and worth of all that is. Christ mysticism is thus a practical, life-centered alternative to the other mythological doctrines of resurrection, ascension, Pentecost, and the Holy Spirit. Christ mysticism is thus, for Paul and for the deeply contemplative while courageously active believers of all generations, the essence of worship.

Two Types of Mysticism

Deissmann, on the basis of studies in the history of religions,[25] distinguishes between two types of mysticism, which are essentially the *quietistic* and the *active*. Deissmann, writing around 1912, was attempting to defend his election of the term "mysticism" and the practice of mysticism against the harsh criticism of the neo-Kantian theological school of Albrecht Ritschl which considered mysticism—along with all "natural theology" to be corruptions of the Christian faith.[26] While the Ritschlian school rejected mysticism because of some mystics' claim to knowledge of God through direct, immediate perception (and/or experience), precisely because their Kantian philosophy denied that any rational (pure or scientific) knowledge of God was possible, the whole idea of mysticism was distasteful to the "critical" mind of most European scholars at the turn of the century. Deissmann, however, had been captured by the evidence he discovered in the Pauline material: Paul was a mystic.[27] How could Deissmann recommend Christ mysticism in such a theological period? How could he understand it himself as a constructive element in the life of the modern church? Deissmann found that the answer was prima facie in the text: Paul's Christ mysticism was a socially active style of life. Paul's religion was no retreat into the hills or desert. Paul's faith was no escape from the turmoil of the world about him; rather, Paul's faith led him forth into the great world of the Mediterranean basin, to work, struggle, and proclaim the Christ event. Paul was thus a model —in his mysticism—for the socially concerned Christian of the twentieth century. Therefore Deissmann was able to convince many Christians to reevaluate mysticism's place in the church. Among those who accepted an active Christ mysticism were Albert Schweitzer,[28] Rudolf Otto,[29] and Paul Tillich.[30]

In many respects, Deissmann's recovery of the important place of mysticism in Christianity was also a recovery of the major stream of Christian tradition, at a time when liberalism had overlooked much of that tradition. Deissmann, we would claim, made it possible to reclaim the mystical tradition of the Middle Ages as well as the Logos Christology of the primitive church.

A New Basis for the New Theology

This last claim needs to be explained, for we do not usually think of Paul's Christology as a Logos Christology (John, ch. 1). Our understanding of the kind of theology that may embrace both a Christ mysticism and a Logos Christology is essentially a Tillichian view, or a reasonable development therefrom. The basic elements of such a new understanding of the oldest (Pauline, Johannine) Christology of Christianity are (1) the understanding of "God" as the Ground of Being, the source of all that is and all that lives; (2) the understanding of "creation" which sees all things as infused with the Divine Immanence (Spirit), from which nothing (organic or inorganic) is separated in fact, but from which human beings may be separated by "alienation" or a lack of awareness of the Divine Ground; (3) the understanding of Christ as the Divine revealer or uncoverer of this situation of our divine grounding; and (4) the description of this Christ function of making man aware of the divine by using the Logos terminology. The Logos is, then, the human agent who is aware of his participation in God fully and completely. The Logos—or Christ—is thus completely "Spirit-filled," and is also aware of his involvement in the "creation," i.e., the constitution of the very universe itself. And, what is most important in the modern situation, this Logos, this Spirit, this Christ, was—and is—fully human. It is in this world (i.e., the universe that man inhabits) that he has come into being and into awareness, and it is in this world that he continues to function as the deepest portion of the spirits of men, who, like him, are also "made in the image of God." This Logos, this Spirit-Christ, now lives, and we now experience him, through other people who bear him as bodies bear diseases or minds bear thoughts. He is our eternal contemporary and will come into our own consciousness, "to dwell with us" (John 14:18–24), when we become aware of his presence in our own experience as well as aware of his activity throughout history. We, too, bear him when, having become aware of his power, we become agents of reconciliation and forgiveness. We, too, do his work (John 14:12–17) when we strive to evolve a social system that has the power to expand to include the uniqueness of every individual, rather than the weakness of contracting to exclude human uniqueness. We, too, are bearers of the Spirit-Christ as well as bearers of the new mentality when we grope for ways of disciplining ourselves that will preserve life and the continuity of life's processes without blighting freedom's creative glibness and disorder.

Such a life of Christlikeness is a tall order. Without being sanctimonious, we may confess that no single individual has the insight, awareness, and power within himself to become such a "Christian man." We can become bearers of the Spirit-Christ only when we have been so grasped by the problems and needs of the men around us, and of their wonderful dignity and awful, latent powers, that we see Christ in every human face. We can, in short, become bearers of the Spirit only in the same way we become bearers of the new mentality, through participation with human beings in human groups. A creative, dynamic Christ mysticism will grow up in us, as a dimension of human awareness, only through the human sensitivity we attain by our knocking about in the world with all kinds of men and women, in every kind of human situation.

As Altizer has prophesied, we find the sacred only in the midst of the secular; or, as Feuerbach has suggested, we find God only when we find man. To call theology and/or Christology "anthropology" may sound weird and heretical to many, until they remember that the Biblical tradition declares that we know God only through the one man, Jesus Christ, who perfectly manifested him. In becoming aware, then, of the Divinity in man, we today may again become aware of the humanity in God—as once before, the humanity of Jesus brought the experience of the Divine into human history. The "measured space" we all search for in which to order our lives and free ourselves for creativity and fellowship then reveals itself as the surface of the earth (or the moon or Mars or anywhere that man may establish himself) where, in the give-and-take of human life, He whom no ear has heard nor eye seen may be indirectly surprised shining through the eyes and sounding through the voices of living, dying, yet self-transcending, men and women like ourselves. The "measured space," the symbol of transcendence, the motivation for programs to overcome hate and prejudice and ignorance and disease and war, is *Dasein* itself, our common humanity—the masque of God.

Jesus' Relation to Other Dasein Revealers

What, if anything, is significantly different about Jesus' historical function as a *Dasein* (or humanity) revealer from the activity and influence of other revealers of the essentials of true humanity who have appeared, from time to time, in human history? Karl Jaspers in *The Great Philosophers* speaks of "men

who by being what they were did more than other men to deter-
mine the history of man. . . . These men are Socrates, Buddha,
Confucius, Jesus."[31] How can we differentiate between the symbol of Jesus and the symbolic power of these and other paradigmatic individuals? Obviously, a distinction between Jesus and
Socrates and the others has been traditionally made, but this
preference of the Jesus symbol has been done on the basis of the
creedal formulas of the institutional churches. We cannot, and
will not, offer the symbol of the Spirit-Christ to Western man
as a live option simply because of the traditional halo painted
over Jesus' head by orthodox Christianity.

If Jesus is herein presented as the primary *Dasein* revealer,
or example of fully developed humanity, it is because of the
pragmatic, empirical status of the Jesus symbol in our culture.
Jesus has been the major symbol of Western humanity's ideals
and aspirations for sixteen hundred years, and this is a fact we
cannot simply ignore. The coming into existence of the new
mentality in all its aspects—political, social, and theological—
is an act of self-transcendence on the part of Western man, not
the destruction of every remnant of the past. That which is still
alive in our heritage will be retained; only that which is dead
(and thus inappropriate to our feelings and unavailable to us on
any level except, perhaps, the sentimental) is rejected. The symbol of "Jesus" is not dead for the bearers of the new mentality
although the pseudo symbols which are used to enhance and
upbuild the figure of Jesus in orthodox theology are dead. The
symbol of Jesus the gentle, the self-denying, the antihero, is still
with us. The symbol of Jesus the King of Glory, the mythical
hero who triumphs over Satan, who comes again in power in the
clouds, is no longer appropriate or available. The efforts of the
New Testament theologians to "demythologize" the Gospel records are simply the tardy activities of verbally (consciously
intellectual) oriented men to do in public what the unconscious
minds of modern men did privately generations ago. Indeed,
Markus Barth's saying is true that men pay their respects to
demythologizing by doing it for themselves.

Just here, the difference between the symbol "Jesus" and the symbolic availability of Socrates, Buddha, Confucius, and other paradigmatic figures becomes clear. As influential as the symbol of Socrates has been in the West, the coming into history of the Jesus symbol prevented Socrates from becoming a basically paradigmatic symbol for the West. Karl Jaspers remarks about the great honor paid to Socrates by the Christian church fathers who saw him as a precursor of the Christian martyrs.[32] But aside from the brilliance of Socrates' light in the Cynic, Cyrenaic, and Platonic schools of philosophy, Socrates has been—perhaps unfortunately—the symbol of the ideal philosopher for Western culture and not the symbol of what every man could and therefore ought to be. In a very real way, history has been unfair to Socrates, for he is, indeed, a Christlike figure symbolizing in an attractive way "the clarity of human possibility."[33] Perhaps the most attractive features of Socrates' personality have been unconsciously assimilated into the symbol of Jesus, for, in all events, it is Jesus and not Socrates who dominates Western history.

In the case of Buddha and Confucius (and other non-Western figures), their paradigmatic importance for great and ancient cultures cannot be denied. However, Buddha and Confucius are paradigmatic figures for Eastern culture, not for the West. We often forget that religion is the spirit of a culture, and thus fall into the shallow belief that a symbol of another religion can be taken over by members of another culture. This is simply psychologically and sociologically impossible, unless the person so "converted" also takes over the culture out of which the symbol arose—and such a complete identification with another culture may itself be an impossibility. The fact that the Jesus symbol is part of Western culture is, therefore, a legitimate reason for holding that Jesus, rather than one of the other *Dasein* revealers of human history, is the symbol most available to the bearers of the new mentality. This is not to practice "religious imperialism" or "cultural imperialism," for this insight cuts both ways; Jesus is not available as a symbol to other cultures in the same manner as he is to ours. The Divine is not limited to one symbol, even if men may be so limited because of the complexities of cultural development.

For the West, the symbol of Jesus Christ may well be the ultimate symbol, the criterion by which all other *Dasein* revealers are judged (as Paul Tillich taught), but what is the case for Western culture need not be considered the case for the Divine. At this point, the relativity of the symbol of Jesus, undoubtedly we touch upon a watershed between the old and the new mentality. For the new mentality, relativity even in the dimension of religious symbols is acceptable and comfortable; for the old mentality, the lack of "security" or absolutism in such a position is frightening and therefore must be rejected. The elements of a new Christology offered here are not to be considered as elements drawn from the established tradition, interpreted in the institutional manner. The touchstone for our approach to Christology is the present, what the symbol of Jesus is capable of performing in the here and now (and perhaps the future). Our touchstone is not the past, and we do not offer the elements of the orthodox tradition we have retained in any spirit of self-justification or out of a desire for theological respectability. The criteria followed here have been phenomenological—a description of what is—at least among some of the younger generations—an appropriate and helpful religious outlook.

The question arises as to how the new symbol of Jesus is to be distinguished from the pseudo symbols and mythological and sentimental accretions around the name of "Jesus" in institutional Christianity. I think there is a simple answer to this, for the way in which the Jesus symbol is and will be used by the bearers of the new mentality will certainly distinguish it from the preaching and other presentations of orthodoxy. To define Jesus as "a place to be" as William Hamilton has done,[34] or to celebrate Communion in private houses in modern argot as the underground church movement is now doing, is to utilize the Jesus symbol in ways that cannot be mistaken for the customs of most institutional forms of Christianity. The development, too, of a new stage in Christ mysticism, with both solitary contemplation and social activism as desirable expressions—which we call for in this book—will also separate the new symbol of Jesus from the verbal patterns of institutional piety and practice.

Possible Developments of Christ Mysticism

In a day of hatreds and tensions at home and abroad, the development of a socially unifying Christ mysticism is a practical as well as a theological necessity. However, no person or small group of persons can develop a symbol or unifying religious cult by itself, for as is the case with great literature, such symbols and traditions must grow out of the experiences of all the people. In the case of the Jesus symbol and devotion to it (mysticism), there are wide areas of human experience within Western culture upon which we can draw. What are these areas? The very areas that trouble our society today, the peace versus war issue, the area of race relations, the struggle to clarify our moral concepts, and the attempts to find firm footings for new progress in philosophy and education.

As an example of this social base, we may remark that the symbol of Jesus will forever remain attached to the movement for racial justice because of the life, work, and martyrdom of Martin Luther King, Jr. Although the stage of the civil rights struggle dominated by Christian leaders and participants is now over (and was essentially over before King's death), the movement will always be marked by King's preaching and the deep response of many black and many white citizens to the religious imagery that King used to call men to brotherhood. A kind of ecstatic Christ mysticism certainly informed the lives of the young Christian Negro students who began the lunch counter sit-ins (and later the kneel-ins) at the beginning of the racial revolution. Something of that spirit is still in the Southern Christian Leadership Conference, although events have largely worn it away. The radical Christian is concerned that the symbol of Jesus become operative again in this significant area of our common life as a substitute for the symbols of hate that have been provoked in many quarters.

The basic thesis of a new form of Christ mysticism is that the figure of Jesus in the Gospels which inspired the symbol of Christ, the perfect man, is not limited to the past, but is operational throughout all of Christian history. The Spirit of Christ is in the world now, diffused throughout the human race, present partially as impulse and goal, in every man. Such a belief in the sacral nature of human personality logically leads on to the acceptance of the moral duty to overcome war and hatred (and all forms of violence and prejudice). It also leads to a demand, on the part of the Christ mystic, for society to redirect its energies away from war and the search for luxuries for some to the utilization of man's resources to fight hunger and poverty.

The implications of this Christ mysticism are that men and women who feel their participation in the universal Christ symbol will redirect their energies away from the institutional church (where the church fails to be concerned) and into new associations for the achievement of Christlike social conditions.

Indeed, many of these implications are already being worked out in the lives of those Christians who are identifying themselves with the so-called underground church. Insofar as this book has uncovered certain problems in our churches and society and has indicated that the cultivation of a new Christ mysticism may be the most constructive effort for the churches to follow, the author also intends to commend the activities of the underground churches. Perhaps in the communion and fellowship of these open and living new spiritual organisms, the past and the future may be brought together in a creative synthesis. Perhaps, too, the old and the new mentality, if brought to a confrontation with each other around the kitchen Communion tables of these new house chapels, might come to understand each other partially. As it is now, the bearers of the old mentality and the bearers of the new inhabit two different worlds. If we are to inhabit any world at all for long, we had best learn to understand each other.

Notes

Preface

1. Charles S. Peirce, "How to Make Our Ideas Clear," *Philosophical Writings of Peirce,* ed. by Justus Buchler (Dover Publications, Inc., 1955), p. 31.

2. *Ibid.*

3. Peirce, "The Concept of God," Buchler (ed.), *op. cit.,* p. 376.

Chapter I. Minds and Mentalities

1. John C. Cooper, *The Roots of the Radical Theology* (The Westminster Press, 1967).

2. Jack Newfield, *A Prophetic Minority* (The New American Library of World Literature, Inc., 1966).

3. *Ibid.,* front of book jacket.

4. Cooper, *The Roots of the Radical Theology,* pp. 16–17 and *passim.*

5. Johann Gottlieb Fichte, "The Science of Knowledge," in *Modern Classical Philosophers,* ed. by Benjamin Rand (Houghton Mifflin Company, 1952), p. 486.

6. *Ibid.*

7. Erik H. Erikson, *Identity and the Life Cycle,* Psychological Issues Monograph Series, Vol. I, No. 1 (International Universities Press, Inc., 1959).

8. Erik H. Erikson, *Young Man Luther: A Study in Psychoanalysis and History* (W. W. Norton & Company, Inc., 1962).

Also see John C. Cooper, "Some Radical Elements in Luther's Theology," *The Lutheran Quarterly,* Vol. XX, No. 2 (May, 1968), pp. 194–201.

9. This description of a college campus is based on a recent visit to a highly respected men's college in the eastern United States.

10. In this book we will use many nonscholarly terms, most of them drawn directly from the daily speech of American young people. "Skuzzy" means dirty or run-down. The political "hippie" is the type that participates in antidraft demonstrations; the dropped-out "hippie" is the type who smokes marijuana and who wants only to pursue his own inner peace.

11. John Cage, *A Year from Monday* (Wesleyan University Press, 1967), p. 166.

Chapter II. Man's Alienation from Traditional Symbols

1. Paul Tillich, *The Dynamics of Faith* (Harper Torchbooks, 1957), pp. 41–54, and "The Religious Symbol," *The Journal of Liberal Religion,* Vol. 2, No. 1 (Summer, 1940).

2. See Carl Gustav Jung, *The Collected Works of C. G. Jung,* Bollingen Series, XX (Pantheon Books, Inc.).

Chapter III. The Death of Western Symbols

1. Ludwig Wittgenstein, *The Blue and Brown Books* (Harper Torchbooks, 1958), p. 68.

2. See Bertrand Russell, *Why I Am Not a Christian and Other Essays,* ed. by Paul Edwards (Simon and Schuster, Inc., Publishers, 1962).

3. Albert H. Friedlander (ed.), *Never Trust a God Over Thirty: New Styles in Campus Ministry* (McGraw-Hill Book Company, Inc., 1967). Malcolm's essay is "The Student Radicals and the Campus Ministry," pp. 71–120.

4. The major writings of the radical theologians are:

a. Thomas J. J. Altizer: *Oriental Mysticism and Biblical Eschatology* (The Westminster Press, 1961); *Mircea Eliade and the Dialectic of the Sacred* (The Westminster Press, 1963); *The Gospel of Christian Atheism* (The Westminster Press, 1966); and William Hamilton, *Radical Theology and the Death of God* (The Bobbs-Merrill Company, Inc., 1966).

b. William Hamilton, *The New Essence of Christianity* (Association Press, 1961).

c. Paul van Buren, *The Secular Meaning of the Gospel* (The Macmillan Company, 1963).

d. Harvey Cox: *The Secular City* (The Macmillan Company, 1965); *On Not Leaving It to the Snake* (The Macmillan Company, 1968).

e. Gabriel Vahanian, *The Death of God* (George Braziller, Inc., 1961).

f. John Charles Cooper: *The Roots of the Radical Theology* (The Westminster Press, 1967); *Radical Christianity and Its Sources* (The Westminster Press, 1968).

5. Cooper, *The Roots of the Radical Theology.*

6. See John C. Cooper, "Ultra-Conservatives and Lutherans Today," *The Lutheran Quarterly,* Vol. XVIII, No. 3 (August, 1966), pp. 214–226.

7. See the entire issue of *The Lutheran Quarterly,* Vol. XVIII, No. 3 (August, 1966), which is devoted to a consideration of "The Church on the Right Wing."

8. This author took part in the Paul Tillich–Mircea Eliade symposium on the relationship of systematic theology and the history of religions at the University of Chicago in 1963–1965.

9. Albert Schweitzer, *Von Reimarus zu Wrede: Eine Geschichte der Leben-Jesu-Forschung* (Tübingen: J. C. B. Mohr, 1906).

10. The first English translation of *The Quest of the Historical Jesus* was made by W. Montgomery in 1910 (The Macmillan Company).

11. The R.E.P., or Radical Education Project, is sponsored by Students for a Democratic Society and is headquartered in Ann Arbor, Michigan.

12. *Ramparts,* now a bimonthly magazine, began its career some years ago as a Catholic news magazine. Now it is probably the best left-of-center publication in the United States. *Ramparts* announced that it was going into bankruptcy in January, 1969.

13. Thomas Luckmann, *The Invisible Religion* (The Macmillan Company, 1967).

14. *Ibid.,* pp. 107–117.

15. See Alfred North Whitehead, *Religion in the Making* (The Macmillan Company, 1956); Bernard E. Meland: *America's Spiritual Culture* (Harper & Brothers, 1948); *The Reawakening of Christian Faith* (The Macmillan Company, 1949); and *Seeds of Redemption* (The Macmillan Company, 1947); Henry Nelson Wieman: *The Issues of Life* (Abingdon Press, 1931); *Religious Experience and Scientific Method* (The Macmillan Company, 1926); and *The Source of Human Good* (The University of Chicago Press, 1946).

16. Richard L. Rubenstein, *The Religious Imagination* (The Bobbs-Merrill Company, Inc., 1968).

17. Ludwig Feuerbach, *The Essence of Christianity* (Harper Torchbooks, 1957).

18. G. W. F. Hegel, *Early Theological Writings* (Harper Torchbooks, 1948).

19. Paul Goodman, in *The Critic,* November, 1967.

Chapter IV. The Post-New Morality

1. Pierre Teilhard de Chardin, *The Future of Man* (Harper & Row, Publishers, Inc., 1963).

2. Delbert L. Earisman, *Hippies in Our Midst* (Fortress Press, 1968), pp. 24–26.

3. *Ibid.,* pp. 28–29.

4. *Ibid.,* p. 65.

5. See John A. T. Robinson, *The Body—A Study in Pauline Theology* (London: SCM Press, Ltd., 1957). Also see John C. Cooper, "The Significance of the Pauline Spirit–Christology for the Doctrine of Spiritual Presence in Paul Tillich," unpublished Ph.D. dissertation, University of Chicago, 1966.

6. Earisman, *op. cit.,* pp. 99 ff.

7. *Britannica Book of the Year 1968* (Encyclopædia Britannica, Inc., 1968), pp. 790–791.

8. *Ibid.,* p. 790.

9. See *LSD on the Campus,* by Warren Young and Joseph Hixson (Dell Publishing Company, Inc., 1966); "Why Students Turn to Drugs," *Reader's Digest,* anonymous, April, 1968; *Campus Values,* ed. by Charles W. Havice (Charles Scribner's Sons, 1968), Ch. 5, pp. 55 ff., *Psychedelics and the College Student,* Student Committee on Mental Health (Princeton University Press, 1967); "LSD, The False Illusion, I & II," (reprint from the FDA papers, September, 1967; Food and Drug Administration, U.S. Department of Health, Education, and Welfare); "Maybe Somebody Else Can Learn from It," J. Anthony Lukas (*Reader's Digest* reprint); and "Bootleg LSD Laboratory," from the Bureau of Drug Abuse Control Bulletin, January, 1967 (U.S. Department of Health, Education and Welfare).

10. Paul Tillich: *The Shaking of the Foundations* (Charles Scribner's Sons, 1948); *The Eternal Now* (Charles Scribner's Sons, 1963); *The New Being* (Charles Scribner's Sons, 1955).

11. Helmut Thielicke: *How the World Began* (Muhlenberg Press, 1961); *The Ethics of Sex* (Harper & Row, Publishers, Inc., 1963); *The Freedom of the Christian Man* (Harper & Row, Publishers, Inc., 1963); *Christ and the Meaning of Life* (Harper & Brothers, 1962), and others.

12. Jean-Paul Sartre, *Being and Nothingness,* tr. by Hazel E. Barnes (Philosophical Library, Inc., 1956), pp. 557 ff.

13. *Ibid.,* p. 575.

14. Poem by John C. Cooper, in *The Holden Courier,* Winter, 1968.

15. *Playboy* panel discussion on "Religion and the New Morality," *Playboy*, Vol. 14, No. 6 (June, 1967), p. 57. Quotations used by permission of Playboy Magazine.

16. *Ibid.*

17. John A. T. Robinson, *Honest to God* (The Westminster Press, 1963), p. 118, italics mine.

18. *Playboy* discussion, *loc. cit.*, p. 57.

19. *Ibid.*, p. 58.

Chapter V. The Search for New Meaning

1. Matthew Arnold, "Dover Beach," *F. T. Palgrave's The Golden Treasury*, rev. ed. by Oscar Williams (Mentor Books, The New American Library of World Literature, Inc., 4th printing, 1959), p. 401.

2. Alfred, Lord Tennyson, from "In Memoriam," Pt. LIV, *The Mentor Book of Major British Poets*, ed. by Oscar Williams (Mentor Books, The New American Library of World Literature, Inc., 1963), p. 235.

3. Alfred, Lord Tennyson, from "In Memoriam," Pt. CVI, F. T. Palgrave, *op. cit.*, p. 383.

4. Algernon Charles Swinburne, "The Garden of Proserpine," *Collected Poetical Works* (Harper & Brothers, n.d.), Vol. I, p. 171.

5. Wilfred Owen, "Dulce et Decorum Est," *Modern British Poetry*, ed. by Louis Untermeyer (Harcourt, Brace & Co., 1950), pp. 359–360.

6. See Warren Young and Joseph Hixson, *LSD on the Campus*.

7. As described by Paul Tillich, *The Courage to Be* (Yale University Press, 1952) and *The Dynamics of Faith*.

8. *Time*, April 5, 1968, p. 61.

9. Jack Kerouac, *On the Road* (Signet Books, The New American Library of World Literature, Inc., 1958).

10. Henry David Thoreau, *Walden, or Life in the Woods* (1854).

11. The terms "doves" and "hawks" supposedly originated among the advisers of the late President John F. Kennedy during the Cuban missile crisis.

12. See *Report of the National Advisory Commission on Civil Disorders* (E. P. Dutton & Company, Inc., 1968).

13. H. Neill McFarland, *The Rush Hour of the Gods* (The Macmillan Company, 1967).

14. See "A Visit with India's High-powered New Prophet," *Look,* Vol. V, No. 32 (February 6, 1968), pp. 64–78.

15. Maharishi Mahesh Yogi, *Meditations of Maharishi Mahesh Yogi* (Bantam Mini Book Special, May, 1968).

16. *Ibid.,* especially pp. 45–50.

17. *Ibid.,* pp. 132–133.

18. The following is a bibliography of works on Zen Buddhism that will aid the interested reader:

Dumoulin, Heinrich, *A History of Zen Buddhism*. London: Faber & Faber, Ltd., 1963.

Frazier, Allie, *Buddhism* (Vol. II of *Readings in Eastern Religious Thought*). The Westminster Press, 1969.

Graham, Dom Aelred, *Zen Catholicism*. Harcourt, Brace and World, Inc., 1963.

Herrigel, Eugen, *Zen*. McGraw-Hill Book Company, Inc., 1964.

Humphreys, Christmas, *Zen: A Way of Life*. Emerson Books, Inc., 1965.

Lao Tzu, *The Way of Life: Tao Te Ching,* tr. by R. B. Blakney. The New American Library of World Literature, Inc., 1955.

Miura, Isshū and Sasaki, Ruth Fuller, *The Zen Koan*. Harcourt, Brace and World, Inc., 1965.

Senzaki, Nyogen and McCandless, Ruth Strout, *Buddhism and Zen*. Philosophical Library, Inc., 1953.

Stryk, Lucien, and Ikemoto, Takashi, eds. and trs., *Zen:*

Poems, Prayers, Sermons, Anecdotes, Interviews. Doubleday & Company, Inc., 1965.

Suzuki, D. T., *The Essentials of Zen Buddhism.* E. P. Dutton
& Company, 1962.

———— *Zen Buddhism: Selected Writings of D. T. Suzuki,* ed.
by William Barrett. Doubleday & Company, Inc., 1956.

———— *The Training of the Zen Buddhist Monk.* University
Books, Inc., 1965.

———— *Zen Buddhism and Psychoanalysis,* ed. by Erich
Fromm and Richard De Martino. Harper & Brothers, 1960.

———— *Studies in Zen,* ed. by Christmas Humphreys. Philosophical Library, Inc., 1955.

———— *Manual of Zen Buddhism.* Grove Press, Inc., 1960.

Watts, Alan W., *The Way of Zen.* The New American Library of World Literature, Inc., 1957.

———— *The Spirit of Zen.* Grove Press, Inc., 1958.

Wood, Ernest, *Zen Dictionary.* Philosophical Library, Inc.,
1962.

Chapter VI. The Revitalization of Traditional Symbols

1. Albert Camus, *The Rebel,* tr. by Anthony Bower (Vintage
Books, Random House, Inc., 1956). See Thomas Hanna, *The
Thought and Art of Albert Camus* (Gateway edition, Henry
Regnery Company, 1958).

2. Jean-Paul Sartre, *Existential Psychoanalysis,* tr. by Hazel
E. Barnes (Gateway edition, Henry Regnery Company, 1965).

3. Jean-Paul Sartre, "Existentialism Is a Humanism," in *Existentialism from Dostoevsky to Sartre,* ed. by Walter Kaufmann
(Meridian Books, The World Publishing Company, 1956).

4. See Pierre Thévenaz, *What Is Phenomenology? and Other
Essays,* ed. by James M. Edie and tr. by James M. Edie *et al.*
(Quadrangle Books, Inc., 1962), pp. 28–29.

5. *Encyclopædia Britannica,* Vol. 15, p. 24.

6. See Thévenaz, *op. cit.*

7. *Ibid.,* pp. 28–29.

8. Nicolas Berdyaev, *The Meaning of the Creative Act,* tr. by Donald A. Lowrie (Collier Books, 1962), p. 285.

9. *Ibid.,* p. 88. "The new Christological anthropology must reveal the secret of man's creative calling and thus give to man's creative impulses a high religious meaning."

10. Friedrich Nietzsche, *The Philosophy of Nietzsche* (Modern Library, Inc., 1954), esp. pp. 75–78, 261, 297, 469, 668–711, 828–829, 908–933.

11. See Cooper, *The Roots of the Radical Theology,* pp. 141–144; Feuerbach, *The Essence of Christianity,* and *Principles of the Philosophy of the Future,* tr. by Manfred H. Vogel (Library of Liberal Arts, The Bobbs-Merrill Company, Inc., 1966).

12. Quietism is the religious attitude toward the world that grows out of an intense turning inward of the spiritual impulse, and that tends to forget the believer's responsibility to be a good citizen of the world. It prizes prayer and "spiritual" things, and neglects the government of society. It is best seen in the Amish, but is widespread as a basic belief among Lutherans and other Christians in the German tradition of pietism (such as the Moravians).

13. A pericope is a short segment of a Gospel, complete in itself. The story of the Gentile woman's encounter with Jesus in Mark 7:25–30 is a pericope.

14. Phil. 1:20–21, from *Good News for Modern Man* (American Bible Society, 1966).

15. Carl Gustav Jung, *The Collected Works of C. G. Jung,* and *Symbols of Transformation,* Vol. I (Harper Torchbooks, 1956). The latter is the same as *The Collected Works of C. G. Jung,* Vol. 5, No. XX of the Bollingen Series.

16. "Docetic"—from the Greek word meaning "to seem to be." Docetism (an early Christian heresy) taught that the Christ only seemed to be a man, but in reality was not. Christ could not be human, Docetism held, because the flesh is evil. This was an extreme form of Greek (Platonic) dualism.

17. "Gnostic"—from the Greek word meaning "knowledge"

(*gnōsis*). Gnosticism is a loose, generic term for a group of religious movements in the first four Christian centuries, which taught that a man is "saved" by the possession of spiritual knowledge. Gnosticism influenced and was influenced by early Christianity as well as influencing Neoplatonism. See Hans Jonas, *The Gnostic Religion* (2d ed., rev.; Beacon Press, Inc., 1963).

18. For the concept of the imitation of Christ, see Thomas à Kempis, *The Imitation of Christ*, tr. by Leo Sherley-Price (London: The Penguin Classics, 1954).

19. See William James, *The Will to Believe, and Other Essays* (Dover Publications, Inc., 1956).

20. Robert Browning, "Andrea del Sarto," in *F. T. Palgrave's The Golden Treasury*, rev. ed. by Oscar Williams (Mentor Books, The New American Library of World Literature, Inc., 1959).

21. Altizer, *Oriental Mysticism and Biblical Eschatology*, pp. 79–112; especially see his *The Gospel of Christian Atheism*.

22. Gerard Manley Hopkins, *Poems and Prose of Gerard Manley Hopkins*, ed. by W. H. Gardner (Penguin Books, Inc., 1964).

23. Kenneth Scott Latourette, *A History of Christianity* (Harper & Brothers, 1953), pp. 78, 135, 137, 143.

24. Adolf Deissmann, *Paul: A Study in Social and Religious History* (Harper Torchbooks, 1959). First edition in German, 1912. See also Cooper, "The Significance of Pauline Spirit-Christology."

25. Deissmann, *op. cit.*, pp. 147–157.

26. See Wilhelm Herrmann, *The Communion of the Christian with God*, tr. by J. S. Stanyon (London, 1898).

27. Deissmann, *op. cit.*, p. 147.

28. See Albert Schweitzer, *The Mysticism of Paul the Apostle*, tr. by William Montgomery (London: A. & C. Black, Ltd., 1953).

29. See Rudolf Otto, *The Idea of the Holy*, tr. by John W. Harvey (Oxford University Press, 1946).

30. See Paul Tillich, *Systematic Theology,* Vols. II and III (The University of Chicago Press, 1957 and 1963).

31. Karl Jaspers, in *The Great Philosophers,* ed. by Hannah Arendt and tr. by Ralph Manheim (Harcourt, Brace and World, Inc., 1962).

32. *Ibid.,* p. 28.

33. *Ibid.,* p. 31.

34. Hamilton, *op. cit.,* pp. 119–122.